Carrie M. Gentry

A LIFE
WORTH LIVING

A Biography of
Howard C. Gentry, Sr.
(1921~1995)

by
Carrie M. Gentry

Printed by R.H. Boyd Publishing Corporation
Nashville, Tennessee
™ R.H Boyd Company

A Life Worth Living
Copyright © 2010 by R.H. Boyd Publishing Corporation, Nashville, TN

6717 Centennial Blvd.
Nashville, TN 37209

ISBN 1-58942-390-9

Printed in the United States of America

Carrie M. Gentry
A Life Worth Living

Dedication

This biography is dedicated to our children, Carol and Howard, and also to the many athletes and others whom my husband embraced with love and caring as if they, too, were his own children.

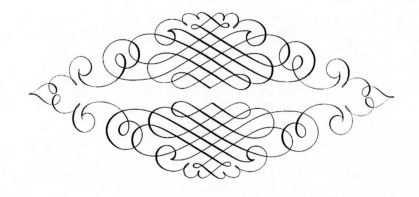

Contents

**Pictures are taken from archived newspaper articles
and family collections.**

Acknowledgments

My heartfelt thanks to my daughter-in-law, Sharon. Her time, insight, diligence, and technical skills in changing my handwritten words into a more suitable condition were absolutely invaluable to me.

Acknowledgements and many thanks are given to my friend, Helen Fouche', and to my granddaughter-in-law, Tiffany Johnson. They appeared like miracles, volunteering their time and talents in helping to get this writing into its final form.

Also, the critical judgments and literary suggestions offered by Pamela Foster, Andrea Blackman, Dwight Lewis, and Yvonne Clark were most helpful and earnestly appreciated.

— Carrie M. Gentry (2010)

Preface

This story is the biography of my husband. He has a building named after him, and it is located on the campus of Tennessee State University in Nashville, Tennessee. It is named the Howard C. Gentry Health, Physical Education, Athletic and Convocation Center.

My motivation to write this story grew out of the fact that numerous persons, who did not know him, have asked why the building was given his name. Consequently, as the story unfolds, it is my hope that one may learn of the unique qualifications that caused him to deserve such an honor. As a matter of fact, this book will introduce to the world a man who, in spite of the obstructions caused by segregation and inequalities, made a tremendous positive mark on the lives of many. And with this historic presentation, those now living, as well as future generations, will, without a doubt, be equally inspired. The story touches upon the entire inspirational and legendary life of Howard Gentry, from his birth in Columbus, Ohio, in 1921, until his death in Nashville, Tennessee, in 1995.

I would like to share the fact that my husband lived during a period of time in history when a specific segment of the population was deprived of many of the advantages that were available to others. When thinking of this, one has to admit that it was truly remarkable that anyone could withstand such inequities and ultimately go on to become successful in life.

Nevertheless, it will be seen that, even though growing up in a poor environment and encountering numerous roadblocks, my husband was fortunate to have been surrounded by his caring family, friends, teachers, and coaches. Their positive influences motivated him to develop into the kind of person who was able to counteract the negative influences that most definitely did exist. Consequently, with their encouragement, he became a person who possessed the determination to be the best that he could be in all of his undertakings—no matter that, many times, the conditions were less than ideal.

Incidentally, his family lived in the Hilltop Section of Columbus on Oakley Avenue. Their house was located right across the street from the Oakley Avenue Baptist Church. I learned that he and his family were constant attendees and one of his older brothers was a deacon in the church. Without a doubt, his having been surrounded by such positive, caring, and spiritual persons during his early years caused him to be motivated to become the kind of exceptional, capable, and spiritual person I knew him to be.

Relative to his personal life, it was evident that he loved his family, his church, his friends, and his community, and he also showed love and concern for all others who were sent his way. Shortly after arriving in Nashville to begin his work at Tennessee State University, and upon his encouragement, we joined First Baptist Church Capitol Hill. From that time until his death, he was an active member. He held membership roles in various committees, and over the years, he held chairmanships on some of them. Kelly Miller Smith, the Civil Rights activist, was the minister of that church.

As the story unfolds, it touches upon the entire life of Howard C. Gentry, Sr.—his early life, his days in elementary school, junior high school, senior high school, college, the army, and his professional career in the fields of education. It tells of his becoming a teacher, a head baseball coach, and an assistant football coach, serving for two years under William Bell at A&T (Agricultural and Technical College in Greensboro, North Carolina). Afterward, he became an assistant football coach for one year under Gaston "Country" Lewis at Wilberforce State College in Wilberforce, Ohio. However, it was in the summer of 1949 when the two of us and our six-month-old daughter arrived on the campus of Tennessee State University in Nashville, Tennessee. It was there that for 27 years he persevered in his subsequent job responsibilities. Over those years there were many heart-rending challenges that confronted him, but he tackled them, which resulted in many joyful and satisfying accomplishments.

Upon his arrival at TSU, his major responsibilities were to teach health and physical education and to act as an assistant football coach under Henry Arthur "The Fox" Kean. He was also given the responsibility of heading up the intramural program. During the same period of time, he assumed many other duties that needed to be performed in order to carry out different programs envisioned by the university's president. No matter what jobs were assigned to him, he tackled each with the same amount of interest and enthusiasm.

For seven years after his arrival at TSU, my husband thoroughly enjoyed working under Coach Kean. Unfortunately, Coach Kean became ill and was unable to continue coaching. Consequently, a decision was made to select one of the assistant coaches to temporarily assume the responsibilities of the head coach. As it turned out, the method used to select the assistant coach, who would become the temporary chairman of the coaching committee, resulted in my husband being chosen. During that season under his leadership, the football team continued to win, thus continuing to do its part in contributing to what became known as the "Golden Era of Athletics" at TSU.

The following year my husband was named Head Coach. The team won all of its games, and they were selected to play in the Orange Blossom Classic in Miami, Florida. Their opponent was his alma mater, Florida A&M University, and its coach was one of his former coaches, the renowned Jake Gaither. After a fierce and competitively-fought game, TSU won. The team became the Negro Champions for that year, and my husband was named Coach of the Year.

The years that followed were exciting and enjoyable. Most of the games were won, and lasting friendships were developed. Also, coaches and others from rival schools were frequent visitors in our home and, likewise, when we would travel, we were welcomed into theirs.

Each year when the members of the football team would return for the preseason practices, it was tradition for them to gather in the backyard of our home for fellowship and a weenie roast. It was heartwarming to see the love and friendship that existed among the players and their coach. During all of the years after the players' graduations, they never lost touch with my husband. When they would return in large numbers for the homecoming games they would always be welcomed into our home for a get-together and dinner and to again view the film of the 1956 Orange Blossom Classic Championship football game.

After serving as a successful coach for five years, 1956-1961, my husband was selected to become the Athletics Director at Tennessee State University. He remained in that position for 15 years. During those years, he proved to be an exceptional director. While promoting and enhancing the programs that were already in operation, he directed the upgrading and expansion of the athletic facilities, thus making it possible for more athletic teams and activities to be added, including the expansion of the intramural program. The Governor's Summer Youth Program and the National Youth Sports Program (NYSP) were initiated. In addition, he became actively involved with the National Association of Collegiate Directors of Athletics (NACDA) and the National Collegiate Athletic Association (NCAA). He held key positions in each—holding chairmanships in the NACDA and a membership on the prestigious NCAA Council.

In 1976, after having worked 27 years at TSU, my husband decided to retire. This he did, but complete retirement did not remain very long. Almost immediately after leaving the campus of TSU, the NCAA asked him to become an evaluator for the NYSP. With his primary desire upon retirement having been to travel and see the United States, he gladly accepted this offer on a part-time basis. For the next seven years, he performed this duty by visiting programs that were conducted on college campuses located all across the country.

Over all the years of my husband's life, there was very little, if any, inactivity. His amazing life was encountered by one unexpected situation after another, with each being of utmost importance. After 10 years of retirement from TSU, he was called back to serve as Interim Athletics Director. One of his major responsibilities while there was to promote TSU's entrance into the Ohio Valley Conference (OVC). After retiring from TSU, he continued to serve on its boards as well as on other committees and boards within his church and with numerous community organizations.

Unfortunately, however, in 1989 an old illness which had been in remission reappeared and a great amount of his activity had to be curtailed. Nevertheless, it was not until 1994 that he finally had to stop, and in the winter of 1995, his life ended.

Many recognitions and honors were bestowed upon my husband during his lifetime. And, undoubtedly, as one reads about them, it will most certainly be understood just why he deserves to have a building named in his honor.

— Carrie M. Gentry

Introduction

"My wife has the habit of going all the way around the universe, so to speak, before ultimately getting back to the point of answering the original question, no matter what it might have been." — Howard C. Gentry, Sr.

I t is the morning of April 16, 2005, and this is the day that I am going to stop procrastinating concerning my desire to write about my life with my husband Howard C. Gentry, Sr.—a life that I shared with him for three months short of forty-eight years.

The question may arise as to why I feel compelled to do this. Well, one reason I will state at this time and another reason will follow later.

The first reason is this: When my husband and I retired, we said that we were going to write about some of the episodes that had occurred in our lives—some wonderful and some maybe not so wonderful. As we talked about doing this, we agreed that the writings would describe our lives from childhood up to the present. Also, we planned to write about additional happenings that we felt most certainly might occur in the future as we traveled through our retirement years.

Speaking of travel, we planned to travel a lot, and we did. We included this plan to travel in our retirement activity because from the time that we started to seriously talk about retiring until we actually did retire, my husband's constant statement went like this: "I want to see the United States and other places of interest before I die." As a matter of fact, his job responsibilities had required him to do a lot of traveling, but he had not had the time to see very much in the places where he had been.

Because we retired at such early ages (my husband was 55 and I was 52), some people expressed the thought that one of us must have been ill. But the fact is that, at the time, neither of us was ill. In reality, however, early retirement was the fulfillment of a desire that had been springing up in my husband's mind years before.

As it happened, shortly after we arrived at Tennessee A&I (presently known as Tennessee State University), Coach Kean, the Head Football Coach, encouraged my husband to take out a retirement policy as he himself had taken one out from an insurance agent. This policy was set up to mature when my husband would become 55 years of age, thus, his introduction to the thought of early retirement.

Fortunately, within that same period of time, the state of Tennessee passed a law whereby those having worked for the state for 30 years and who were 55 years of age could retire with benefits. When my husband turned 55, he and I had worked at A&I for only 27 years. However, with my husband having served in World War II, he had the opportunity to add three of those military years to the twenty-seven causing him to have enough years to retire with benefits.

But then came the question, "What about me?" He had always thought of our retiring at the same time and of our using our retirement years to see the world together. But I only had 27 years of employment. Consequently, I could not retire with benefits.

Well, he set about to work it out on paper, whereby—since we were known to be frugal—we could live on just his income with the plan being for me to vest. This meant that my retirement would be left in the system for the next three years (at which time I would become 55 years of age) and then I could start drawing my retirement.

My husband chose to elect the Social Security Leveling Option. This plan would allow him to be paid, in addition to his retirement, a part of his Social Security which he ordinarily would not get until he reached age 62. Of course, at that time, his Social Security amount would be reduced. But as he visualized it, I would then be drawing my retirement, thus causing the reduction to be inconsequential.

As he excitedly showed me his paperwork, he made mention of how each future period would first bring in my retirement benefits, followed by the Social Security benefits—noting how these increments would take care of inflation. And then, knowing the thrifty people that we were, he said that after that time, we would not need any more money!

In the midst of his showing such excitement about his opportunity to retire and the possibility of my resigning, I made mention (even though I was reluctant to say so for I did not want to burst his bubble) of the fact that if he should predecease me within the next three years and if I should resign, I would be without a job and without an income. Having brought this truth to his attention, he went back to the drawing board with the determination to take care of this situation. He readjusted his retirement plan to the extent that if he should predecease me, I would receive a part of his retirement. In order to have this take place, he could not, at the same time, use the Social Security Leveling Option. This he accepted, for it was more important to him for me to be able to resign to travel with him and to have a certain amount of future security than it was to have more income at that particular time.

So, after having worked at TSU for 27 years, my husband retired and I resigned in November 1976. Upon leaving the university, we set out to travel over the highways and byways of the United States (including Hawaii), Mexico, and Canada. Our mode of travel was sometimes by air and other times in our car. But most of the time we traveled in our motor home, and we joyfully went in whichever direction the winds would blow us. If traveling by car or motor home, we would continuously enjoy viewing the beautiful countryside. And in keeping with our plan of writing about things that had occurred in our lives, we would talk about our past experiences, and as one would drive the other would write. These were glorious times, which we felt blessed to have had the opportunity to experience.

As we continued to write about our past lives and the different experiences we had, new things of interest continued to appear. So there were always subjects of interest about which to write, and this we did. However, we never completed our writings, nor did we put them all together under one cover as we had planned to do. It seemed like something unexpected and, usually, something extremely time-consuming would continuously get in the way, causing our efforts to be thwarted.

For example, in August of 1980, when we returned to Nashville from one of our trips, something totally unexpected happened. My husband and I were in attendance at an activity in the newly-completed Health, Physical Education, Recreation and Convocation Complex. While moving around meeting and greeting friends, Dr. Frederick S. Humphries, the President of TSU (January 1975-June 1986), came to me and whispered into my ear, "We are going to name this building after your husband." I am sure that if a heart could really burst with pride, at that moment, mine surely would have done so!

A few days later, in September of 1980, a letter from the Tennessee Board of Regents was delivered to our home, confirming that the new building was to be named the Howard C. Gentry Health, Physical Education, Recreation and Convocation Complex!

Of course, and above all, we wanted to write about this tremendous honor as well as about many other things that continued to occur in our lives. So, yes, we wrote and we wrote, but seemed never to be able to complete our work.

Time passed and we continued to have enjoyable and fulfilling retirement years. Unfortunately, my husband did become ill, and his untimely death occurred on February 14, 1995.

Since my husband's death, which took place ten years ago, I have spoken many times of wanting to complete some of the things about which we started to write. It, however, has not been until this present time that I made the absolute commitment, in spite of continuous interruptions, to proceed to do this. And, at this time, I will reveal the other reason, which I alluded to earlier, for my making this commitment.

Many times I have been asked and am still being asked this question: "Why was that building on the campus of TSU named after him?" Almost always the ones asking the question have been relatively young individuals or possibly people new to the city who did not know my husband, and, therefore, did not have any knowledge about the life or career of this man. So, the asking of such a question can, most certainly, be understood. I consider this a very valid question—a question that probably a host of other persons might have thought but have not asked.

Previously, in an effort to answer those questions, as I did many times, I would briefly share some of my husband's accomplishments while at TSU—from the time of his arrival in August of 1949 until the end of his tenure in 1976. I would simply say that he served as an exceptional line football coach, teacher of Health and Physical Education, Intramural Director, head football coach, and Director of Athletics.

Presently, however, I feel constrained to answer the question in a way that my husband would often warn people that I would do. He would say, "My wife has the habit of going all the way around the universe, so to speak, before ultimately getting back to the point of answering the original question, no matter what it might have been."

With this thought in mind and because of the importance of the question as well as its value for posterity and others, I feel that I should answer the question in a more detailed manner. I feel that I should take time to chronicle the life of this man, telling who he was and highlighting his significant accomplishments.

It is of utmost importance to also relate how his various experiences helped to shape him into becoming the kind of person he became—the kind of man whose overall performances caused him to achieve such a station in life which resulted in people feeling that he was deserving of having a university building named in his honor. At this point, I also want to state that those constant questions have caused me to decide to deviate from my original plan of completing all of the various writings which my husband and I had begun—writings about episodes pertaining to both of us. Instead, I feel that I can more adequately answer the questions about him by having this writing to be primarily about Howard C. Gentry, Sr. with the majority of other writings to follow at a later time.

I can do this writing about my husband because of my possession of taped interviews, and newspaper and magazine articles about him and because of conversations I had with him, as well as conversations with members of his family and numerous friends and acquaintances. I remember a great deal of the content of these talks and will certainly write about them. It is also important to note that I have in my possession many written pages of information about him that he dictated.

I also have a set of tapes that contain extensive information regarding his life. These particular tapes were created a number of years after my husband's retirement. It was in 1984, when Arthur Ashe, the tennis icon, was in the process of writing a volume of books that a call was made to my husband from the office of Arthur Ashe. The caller asked if my husband would share with him and Arthur Ashe his knowledge and his personal experiences involving his participation in the athletic arena. He especially wanted to discuss my husband's long number of years of dealing with athletics in black colleges and universities. And he wanted to have a discussion with my husband regarding his knowledge of black athletes in other performance areas. Of course my husband readily agreed. So a person by the name of Kip Branch was sent from Arthur Ashe's office to our home in Nashville to carry out this purpose.

Mr. Branch arrived early one morning, and they conversed that whole day. Athletics, in black colleges and universities, were the major topics discussed, but the conversations constantly veered from those subjects to topics covering a large number of other ideas concerning athletes in other venues and other situations dealing with life in general. Mr. Branch wanted to hear about my husband's early years as well as many other experiences throughout his life. When the day ended and as Mr. Branch prepared to leave, he promised to send copies of the tapes upon which their conversations were recorded, and this he did.

Since these tapes contain so much information that over the years may be lost to the memory, I consider them to be prized possessions as I proceed with the effort to answer the questions asked of me regarding the qualifications of Howard C. Gentry, Sr. As a matter of fact, I am going to transcribe in this biography a great deal of the questions and answers from that day as they can be heard on the tapes. In addition, I will include some of my husband's personal writings as well as some of his specific dictations to me.

As I make use of the various pieces of information I have gathered, researched, and spread out across the whole floor of a room, I have a tendency to want to write primarily about the good and happy times in his life, and certainly there were many of those. But, in reality, this would not be the complete story. I can recall that in many of his conversations he acknowledged that he encountered quite a few bad, undesired happenings. As we know, the environment, the people in it, and the period of time in which we live more than likely will influence the kinds of situations that might occur. Sometimes they are good and sometimes they are bad. Of importance, however, is how individuals react to the situations.

As for my husband and how those situations affected him, I heard him say that some of those negative experiences resulted in being important, positive, motivational milestones as he traveled the road to maturity and ultimately to adulthood. He said that in some instances, those negative happenings caused him to make positive decisions as to how he would attempt to conduct his life, especially in the areas of academics and athletic efforts. He said that as he matured, he knew that he wanted to be successful in whatever he chose to do; he developed the attitude that under all circumstances, good or bad, he was going to strive to be the best that he could be. It was this kind of attitude and determination that took him through many stages of his life. Over the years, it was his exceptional performance that caused him to be sought after and ultimately led to his being brought to TSU.

Beginning with a description of my husband's birth, the following chapters will chronicle detailed episodes, activities, and professions that will provide significant insight into the life and character of this man. It is my hope that this knowledge about him will cause one to admire him as I do. And most importantly, it is my hope that the information presented in this biography will adequately answer the question as to why the building was named the Howard C. Gentry Health, Physical Education, Recreation and Convocation Complex.

THE HOWARD GENTRY COMPLEX: Located on the main campus of Tennessee State University

CHAPTER ONE

Infancy and Childhood Days

"As a young child growing up in a large family numbering eight children, life was difficult, to say the least." — *Howard C. Gentry, Sr.*

It was on April 15, 1921 in Columbus, Ohio when James and Della Gentry became proud parents of their seventh child. He was a bouncing baby boy whom they named Howard Cornelius. But as fate would have it, when he was about two years old, he became ill with meningitis and the doctor said that he could not recover. Even though there was a high rate of infant mortality in those days, his father, as I was told, was a man of great faith, and he would not accept the doctor's prediction. Instead, he got on his knees and prayed and prayed for his child to be spared. Afterward, the father announced that his baby was not going to die and that he was going to grow up and become a great teacher.

Obviously, this child did not die. And, as this story about him unfolds, it will be brought to light that just as his father predicted, he did grow up and he did become a teacher. This boy would also one day be a great positive influence upon the many students and other persons with whom he would come in contact.

Also, while in his childhood, he acquired the nickname "Tubby." Although it was common knowledge why his family, friends, and acquaintances called him Tubby, I am sure that the number of times I was asked how he got that nickname greatly outnumbered the number of times I was asked why that building was named after him.

Each time I was asked, I answered the question in the way that it was told to me. According to my husband, his father worked for a railroad company cleaning cars, and he found a dirty little doll with the name "Tub Tillie" written on it. My husband said that his father brought it home and gave it to him. My husband said that he became extremely attached to that little doll—hugging it and hardly ever putting it down, thus, causing his family and others to start calling him Tubby. This nickname stuck with him, and it never left. In my husband's own words:

As a young child growing up in a large family numbering eight children, life was difficult, to say the least. I was three years old when Papa died and my youngest sister was three months of age. The oldest child was a freshman, attending Ohio State University, and the next oldest child was a senior in high school. Due to the fact that my father had a menial type job, cleaning cars for the Norfolk and Western railroad, he only made enough money for this large family to get by on. It was a difficult time for my mother who only had a sixth grade education and had never worked outside of the home. As was to be expected, she applied for the widows' pension but was denied compensation because she refused to take her daughter out of college as well as refused to send some of the other children to live with aunts and uncles in the greater Columbus area. Because of her not taking their suggestions, she was denied aid and she decided that she would do whatever was necessary to keep her family together.

[Because] the three younger children were not of school age, it was impossible for her to leave the house in search of employment. To bring in some money to take care of expenses, she took into the home washing and ironing clothes for persons living on the Hilltop, the area in which we lived.

The oldest male at the time of father's death was only 12 years old, but he immediately felt the responsibility by seeking employment of any type of job that he could get. My oldest sister, who was in college, remained in school but did whatever she could to help support the family. The second oldest child ran off and got married to a mail carrier who lived in Jamestown, Ohio. God only knows how we survived, but we had a strong mother who stated, "Where there is a will, there is a way!"

I remember that my grandmother and my grandfather lived on a farm. At hog killing time, my mother would go to the farm and come back home with a side of pork which was hung on the back porch where it was very cold. This would keep it from spoiling. Also, I remember that she would bring back a five-gallon container of buttermilk fresh from the churn. During the summer, the entire family would work in the gardens which provided fresh vegetables for our family as well as for others in the community who were in need.

When I got to be of school age, my mother would take me to the farm where I remained most of the summer. Fond memories remain of my grandmother who spent her time working in the garden and preparing food for the work hands. As a youngster, I remember working with her in the garden pulling weeds. This little lady worked me to death! How I longed to be able to work in the fields with the older boys and my uncles. At times, I felt that it would be the only method for my survival!

As a youngster, as well as to the present time, I have had difficulty keeping my pants up due to the fact that I have no hips. When my grandmother would notice that my pants were slipping down, she would get apron strings and pin them to the back of my britches and would cross them over my shoulders and pin them to the front of my britches. I guess she kept safety pins with her for emergencies like this. While others called me by my name or my nickname Tubby, she called me Jigo. None of the family, as well as myself, knew where she got that name!

As for Grandpa, he was a very stern individual and a man of few words. I remember his inviting me to ride to town with him in his buggy to take care of some business at the mill one morning. From the time that I got in the buggy until the time that we got back to the farm, he spoke only four words, and those were spoken when we got to the mill and they were, "Stay in the buggy." Though he was not much of a talker, he was a good man, and he loved his family. I was the proudest person in the world to be riding by his side as we made the trip to the mill!

I remember a lot of good times and lots of good food (chicken, green beans, sweet corn on and off the cob, mashed potatoes, tomatoes, ham, beef, buttermilk, pies and cakes, ice cold lemonade, etc.). But as I became older, all on the farm was not fun. Chores had to be done. Most of the time a day went like this:

- There was a call from Grandpa before daybreak.
- The horses had to be brought in from the fields. They had to be fed, curried, and brushed.
- The cows had to be brought up for milking.
- The hogs had to be fed.
- There was a half-day's work before breakfast. Breakfast consisted of such foods as hot biscuits, bacon, sausage, ham, milk, butter, jelly, and fried potatoes.
- After breakfast, we went to the fields to work until Grandpa indicated the time for lunch. He made this determination by looking and determining the position of his shadow on the ground.
- After about an hour at lunch, we went back to the field until the sun went down.

We had our heavy meal at noon, and we had supper in the evening. After supper and at dark, Grandma would call all into the living room for prayer. Grandpa would pray for about fifteen minutes, after which he and Grandma would go to bed after which all would retire.

I slept in the loft on straw ticks and, after use, they were lumpy and the straw stuck! After threshing, Grandma would put new straw in the ticks, and they would be a bit more comfortable as I lay on my back and looked up at the stars through the cracks in the roof.

CHAPTER TWO

Elementary School Days

"We would put a board upon a telegraph pole and shoot basketballs. We cleared off all the stuff from the garden spaces, and we played football and softball. We played hockey in the middle of the street, and we just had a good time."

— *Howard C. Gentry, Sr.*

As I continue telling about the life of my husband, this section will include the questions and answers found on the tapes received from the office of Arthur Ashe. The following interview was conducted by Kip Branch.

Branch: What were your first days in school like?

Gentry: I remember my first days in school as being very good days, but as the years progressed, I was not a very good student. As a matter of fact, when I got to the sixth grade, they placed me, along with several other children who were not doing well, in a special room, which was commonly known as the "Dumb Room!" I remember well our teacher who gave us special attention with the hope that we might improve.

At that time, they did not fail you but passed you on with the hope of getting you out one way or the other. In an effort to keep us busy, they decided to form a basketball team utilizing only the students who were in this situation. We were given a pair of green shorts and a yellow shirt which was dyed and numbered by teachers and students. [Because] there were several schools in the city that had these special classes, we engaged in competition with each other, and when we played at home, all the students in the schools came out to cheer us on.

This was an important milestone in my life because it was the first time that I had really been recognized for my exceptional ability. I had grown to be a healthy individual and could run, jump, hang, and swing with the other talented youngsters. For the first time, I had a feeling that I was somebody and that if I continued to do well, I could achieve recognition and acclaim from others. For a youngster who had never owned even a pair of skates, let alone a bicycle, the acclaim which I was getting was really something and I felt good!

Branch: So, was that the period of time that you first got interested in athletics?

Gentry: Well, yes and no. First of all, I was one of eleven children. Eight lived to adulthood. My brother, Harry, was an athlete while he attended high school. It was thrilling to me that he played on the football team. When he would bring his football togs home, I would have the joy of putting them on and pretending to be a football player. Further, kids in the neighborhood found ways to play sports activities. You see, we didn't have an organized recreational program in the community. Frankly, I lived in a community of whites, but there was a small number of blacks that lived within a pocket of the community. And, as a youngster, when we would go to the parks, they would run us away.

So, in that little tight community, we would have our own activities. We would put a board upon a telegraph pole and shoot basketballs. We cleared off all the stuff from the garden spaces, and we played football and softball. We played hockey in the middle of the street, and we just had a good time.

So my initial interest in sports came along as a combination of these kinds of activities and seeing my brother participate on West High School's football and basketball teams, and, of course, my experience while participating on the "Dumb Room" basketball team. Together, all of these experiences resulted in my developing a tremendous interest in sports.

Of importance also is the fact that from the time that I was a youngster, I had dreamed of playing football at Ohio State University. Even though I had never seen OSU play, it was more or less an obsession with me that one day I would have a chance to perform in that great stadium! From the beginning, I was so desperate to be a part of that program at OSU that I attempted to join the Boy Scouts, even though I was not old enough to be a member of that organization. There was a local scout troop at my church, but it did not have a Cub Scout program. However, the scoutmaster would let me come to the meetings, where I began to master the first stages of scouting [toward] the Tenderfoot rank. At the first meeting that I attended after I became 12 years old, I was able to get my Tenderfoot badge. Now the real reason for wanting to be a Boy Scout was that by my being in the organization, I would have an opportunity to be an usher at the home Ohio State University football games. But, in order to be an usher, I had to own a Boy Scout uniform. However, due to the financial conditions of my family, my mother could not afford to buy me a uniform.

Many times I expressed to the scoutmaster that I would like to have a uniform so that I could get the opportunity to be an usher. In an effort to help me, he evidently talked it over with his wife and the two of them decided to help. Their youngest son was already an Eagle Scout, so he had some parts of the uniform that they permitted me to use. The next thing they did was to discuss with me the possibility of selling hot rolls to persons in the community each Saturday afternoon. The plan was that the scoutmaster's wife would make the rolls and would also secure the customers and all that I had to do was to deliver these rolls. So, of course, I agreed to do this, and each Saturday after I made my rounds, I would take the money which I had collected back to the scoutmaster's wife. She kept it for me until I had enough to buy another piece of the uniform. It was a happy day when I was finally able to dress out in my complete Boy Scout uniform and to become an usher at the OSU games!

I was thrilled to go to the big games and to watch OSU play football. Also, I was so eager to see what it felt like to be down on the playing field, so much so, [that] after the game ended, I would jump over the wall and run out onto the field and just dream! After graduating from John Burrows Elementary School, I went on to junior high school where I continued to play basketball and added to my athletic activities the sports of track and field.

CHAPTER THREE
Junior High School Days

"Each time that I was involved in trouble, my mother was notified, and 99 percent of the time I received from her a stern response as well as physical punishment."
— Howard C. Gentry, Sr.

 s my husband and Mr. Branch continued the interview, they shifted to my husband's junior high school days.

Branch: What was your life like among all the other students in junior high after having been in the "Dumb Room"?

Gentry: My participation in athletics continued to be enjoyed. However, I remember suffering the humiliation of the segregated environment but this had nothing to do with my having been in the "Dumb Room." The fact is this: Even though us "Coloreds" (as we were known at that time) could attend the schools, we could not participate in the activities that all other students enjoyed. It was not possible for us to be a member of the various school clubs, nor was it possible for us to be associated with white classmates outside of the school environment.

Even though Columbus, Ohio was so-called integrated, Coloreds were denied the opportunity to purchase tickets at most of the theaters. There were three theaters in town that admitted Colored patrons, but the seating was segregated. With regard to the other accommodations that were available to the masses, such as restaurants and hotels, no Colored individuals were allowed to sit down in the restaurants nor to stay in the hotels. Although it was possible for us Coloreds to use the city parks, the persons in charge of the parks continued to discourage us to the degree that often we would leave the park in search of other areas that we could enjoy. Often, those unsupervised activities in which we engaged were of a destructive nature, and in some cases the police were summoned to break up our activities.

I mention all of these things because they point out the difficulty that we had in preparing ourselves for our future role in society. Because we were segregated, we had no one else to visit with and enjoy but ourselves. This caused conflict when we left our environment and encroached upon the surrounding environments. Often, as a result of this separation and the lack of a complete knowledge of the total community, many times fighting between the two communities took place. Each time that I was involved in trouble, my mother was notified, and 99 percent of the time I received from her a stern response as well as physical punishment.

Branch: When did you start participating in football?

Gentry: After junior high school I went to West Senior High School. It was on the campus of that school where I had my first opportunity to try my hand in the game of football.

CHAPTER FOUR
High School Days

"As an athlete, I became well known for my athletic prowess, but as a student obtaining good grades, I was not." — *Howard C. Gentry, Sr.*

Gentry: During my time in high school, I continued to participate in basketball and track and field, but my strongest suit was in football. If you can imagine this, and I am sure that some can, when I went out for the football team, my coach told me that if I wanted to play, I could not be just as good as the others, but I would have to be a whole lot better than my other teammates. Being the only Colored boy on the team, I was determined that I was going to play. My older brother, Harry, played on the football team when he was in high school there, and my dream was to do the same. So, I began playing football with reckless abandon.

During this period of time, another very interesting and important thing happened to me. I believe it was during my first year in high school. The Kappa Alpha Psi Fraternity—incidentally, it so happened that both of my brothers were Kappas—were having a "Guide Rite" meeting over at the Blue Triangle YMCA.

Now in Columbus, I want you to understand that even though it was in the North above the Mason-Dixon Line, it was segregated to a large degree. You could go to schools. They had integrated the schools, but on the other hand, they had a black (Colored) YMCA and they had a white YMCA. They called the Colored YMCA the Blue Triangle YMCA. It was located way across town from where we lived, but my mother got a job there making up beds. It was one of her numerous jobs. So I heard about the "Guide Rite" meeting from her, and since one could ride across town on the streetcar for three cents, I was able to go to the meeting.

The members of the Kappa Alpha Psi Fraternity in the Columbus Alumni Chapter had the "Guide Rite" program, and they invited youngsters to come to this activity for the purpose of trying to encourage them to become interested in going to college. And, of course, I wanted to go to college and I wanted to go to Ohio State University. Upon enrolling in their program, they talked to us about the requirements that individuals needed in order to go to college.

In the schools, blacks coming from the poor black communities like the one in which I grew up, among most of us, they put the girls in home economics, and they put the boys in shop classes. That was where they placed me. So, there again, my mother had to work, and the thing that she was interested in was my being in school. As long as I was in school, she was satisfied. She had no knowledge about the courses that one should take in order to go to college. I found out from that "Guide Rite" program that I could not go to Ohio State because I was not taking the right courses. So I went back to my homeroom, and I told my teacher that I wanted to go to college. Upon my request, they then put me in college preparatory courses. Therefore, I took more mathematics, history, and other courses that I needed. I took foreign language. I remember I took Spanish. I took the courses that would enable me to go to college should the opportunity present itself.

Branch: But you had to do it on your own initiative?

Gentry: Oh, I did it on my own initiative after getting the information from the Kappa "Guide Rite" program. Incidentally, that is probably why I became a Kappa later on.

Branch: Did you have an athletic hero during the time that you were growing up?

Gentry: Yes, I did. Bill Bell was at OSU. He was one of the first black athletes to play football at OSU. He was All-Conference at guard, and I used to hear about him. And right in the same neighborhood, there was Jesse Owens. He was from Cleveland, Ohio. When he came to OSU, he and his family lived right down the street from where my family lived. One of the wonderful experiences I had was that I could sit at my home and watch him pass by going to his home. I used to just marvel at this guy and say that one day I would like to be like him. He was the idol of all the youngsters in my community.

Branch: How much older was he than you at the time?

Gentry: Oh gee. Jesse was in college, and I was still in the grades. So, if the Olympics in which he participated were in 1936, I would have been about 15 or 16 years old.

Branch: What did he mean to you?

Gentry: Well, there again. He was a great athlete at OSU, and everybody looked up to him and this is what I wanted. I wanted somebody to look up to me. This was important to me. I played awfully hard at everything that I did. I kept all the rules and regulations. I did not eat pie and cake because the coach said that it was not good for my health. I did not smoke because the coach said don't smoke. I wanted to be a top athlete like Jesse Owens.

Branch: By this time, were you doing satisfactory school work?

Gentry: As an athlete, I became well known for my athletic prowess, but as a student obtaining good grades, I was not. I remember that I had to maintain a C average to be eligible to participate in sports, and many times I failed to qualify. This inability to be eligible caused coaches and others to be greatly concerned and, therefore, I was given the opportunity to take tests over, and several times my classmates took the tests for me. Of course, as I look back, I acknowledge that this was wrong but, unfortunately, even today, it remains one of the tragedies facing some athletes, but especially the black athlete.

By the time that I became an 11th grader, I was placed on the City All-Star Team. As a senior, I was, again, selected All-City. So, I just knew that I would be offered a scholarship at OSU. I believe I was offered about twenty scholarships when I graduated from high school. In Ohio, there is a college in about every section of the state, and they all wanted at least one black. So, of course, I had many offers, but I wanted to go to Ohio State University.

Branch: Being a member of the City All-Star Team, as well as All-City, did you not get an offer from Ohio State University?

Gentry: The answer is no. And I am sure that it can be understood that after dreaming so long and so hard for the chance to play football at OSU, it was devastating when I was finally able to go to college and was unable to accomplish my dream.

What happened was this. Back in 1939, very few Colored athletes played football or any other sports at Big Ten schools. However, several friends of my older brother who had graduated from OSU very much wanted me to attend their alma mater. So, they got an appointment for us to go to the campus to talk with the Athletics Director about the possibility of my getting a scholarship at Ohio State. The Athletics Director suggested that we should go to see the Head Football Coach. In an effort to have a conference with him, it was very hurtful when he refused to talk with us.

Branch: Why?

Gentry: Well, I think that I might explain it in this way. The last person that the group suggested that we might go to see was the coach of the freshman team. He granted us an interview, but our conference with him also resulted in making me feel very sad.

First, he spoke of the fact that the Colored athletes were poor students and could not do the classwork that was required of them. Secondly, he stated that they already had two or three Colored players, and they did not want additional Colored players at that time.

I feel certain that he, as well as the others who did not choose to waste their time talking to us, thought of the additional problems that would exist because of the segregation laws. I feel that they did not want to maximize the problems. You may not know this, but the Colored athletes who were in the program at the time were denied the opportunity to live on the campus with their fellow students. They were forced to live off campus, as were all other Colored students who were attending Ohio State University. Further, whenever OSU's team went to southern states to participate, the Colored athletes on the team could not make the trip. Nevertheless, the freshman coach did state to us that if a chance should become available for me to become a part of that program that he would call me. Of course, such a call never did come. The disappointment which I suffered continued to be overwhelming.

Branch: Did you accept one of the scholarships that were offered?

Gentry: No. I decided that I would get a job and just go to work.

Branch: What kind of job did you get?

Gentry: My first job was as an elevator operator in one of the buildings downtown. It just so happened that a cousin of my mother had a husband who ran a small business in this building. His name was Ed Burkhead and he helped me to get that job. He had followed my athletic career with great interest, and even today I remember and cherish the several letters of encouragement that he wrote to me during those years.

Even though I was enjoying working as an elevator operator and having contact with Mr. Burkhead, I heard of a job opening at the Deshler Wallick hotel. Since it paid more than I was presently making, I immediately applied for that job, which would make me a doorman at the hotel. They picked me for the job and I think the only reason that they did so was because I was about the same size as the person who held the job previously. I believed that by so doing, it was unnecessary for them to have to buy a new uniform since I could use the same one that the previous door-man had worn.

This was quite a job. First of all, I had to work a split shift which con-sisted of my being there on the door during the morning hours as well as the evening hours. I remember that my responsibilities consisted of greet-ing persons who arrived by car and unpacking luggage from the car or carrying luggage and placing it in the car for guests who were departing. The usual thing that occurred at that point was this: the person receiving the services would give me a tip, which was usually a nickel, dime, quarter or maybe a fifty-cent piece. My response would be a tip of my cap as I said, "Thank you." I want to point out, however, that some of the people that were assisted by me did not always give me a tip, but a tip of the hat and a smile were still in order.

The money on the door was good, and I was very happy to be receiving it. I found out, however, that there were other things that I could do where the tips would be even better, though some of those things might have been a bit unethical. Many times when individuals would be coming to the hotel for lunch or dinner, I would take their keys and double-park their vehicle until they returned. Another profitable enterprise consisted of purchasing liquor from the state store, which was right across the street, and putting it in my locker. The state liquor store closed at six o'clock and many of the hotel guests wanted to buy liquor after that time. They often inquired as to where they could get a bottle and, of course, I would tell them that I could help them. This type of transaction was very lucrative!

Further, there were prostitutes who frequently passed by the door. They would give their personal cards to me, which I would make available to men who would ask where they could go for a good time. The prostitute would come by the next day and put something into my hand. As I said before, the money was good, and I saved quite a bit during the period of time that I was employed in this job.

Branch: How long did you work on that job?

Gentry: As the summer moved on, one evening at the supper table, my older sister, Bertha, asked me where I was going to attend college. My response to her was that I was making more money at the hotel than most men who had families, and I told her that I was not going to college. At this remark, my brother, Harry, broke into the conversation, stating that if I did not take one of the many scholarships that had been offered to me that he would make me go to Ohio State University for which he would pay. At that moment I knew that my tenure on that job was not much longer.

Speaking of scholarships, I had heard from a number of the colleges in Ohio as well as at least five black schools, primarily in the South. But generally, my interest in college had been shattered. In the meantime, Harry had discontinued work toward a degree at OSU, which had consisted of two years of pre-law, and he had gone to work at the Columbus Auto Parts to earn money to help my siblings, Mary, Gertrude, and Joe, attend Bluefield State Teachers College in Bluefield, West Virginia. In addition, Bertha, who was attending OSU, in an effort to provide further assistance for my mother and Harry to pay for the three kids at Bluefield, she left the university after two years. She then began teaching in West Virginia at a school for wayward girls. As for my mother, she had taken a job at the McMillan Sanitarium as a worker in the laundry where she earned 12 dollars a week. She would also work evenings as a cook in a fast food restaurant. The combining of resources enabled the three enrollees at Bluefield State to graduate and to embark upon teaching careers in the state of West Virginia. My mother always told us that our father wanted his children to get as much schooling as possible. So, you can now understand the futility of my stating that I was not going to college! And, also, when Harry spoke, that was the law, and I didn't care to challenge him at that time—even though I had turned 18 and was sort of large of stature.

Even though I was very unhappy that I could not keep on working on the job which I had, I finally decided to attend a college as far away from home as I could get!

Branch: Where did you decide to go?

Gentry: Finally, my choices dwindled down to a school in Tallahassee, Florida—Florida Agricultural and Mechanical College, commonly known at that time as FAMCee and later came to be known as FAMU.

Branch: What caused you to make the decision to go there?

Gentry: The first week in August I received a letter stating that the Head Coach and an assistant would be coming through Columbus and would take me to school if I would decide on their school. The Head Coach was Bill Bell. The same guy, Bill Bell, that I had idolized at OSU some years before. There were some other guys from Columbus at Florida A&M and they had been by to see me earlier. The letter as well as the visits helped to cause me to consider Florida.

But Bill Bell came to see me this particular day. Incidentally, his assistant coach was Alonzo "Jake" Gaither, who later became the great head coach and the Athletics Director at FAMU. It just so happened that they were on a recruiting trip. They had been up in Akron, Ohio, and they had recruited two young men by the names of Macon Williams and Eddie Sherfield. So when they came through Columbus in Jake Gaither's car, they had these two guys in the backseat. Coach Bell and Coach Gaither came into my house and talked to my mother, and she then said that she would allow me to go to Florida. My mother fixed a big meal for all of us, and I recall not having much of an appetite, but I watched Coach Bell, the Head Coach, eat! Boy, could he eat!

Coach William Bell was a football player who had graduated from OSU. He graduated in 1932 and had coached at several schools before he took the job at FAMU. He was quite an athlete, and as I found out in later years, a perfect gentleman. The assistant coach, Jake Gaither, had likewise coached at other schools before going to FAMU. He, too, I learned, was a man of high principles, and I was indeed fortunate, though I did not know it at the time, to have been associated with these two men. So after dinner, they packed me up, and with very little more than what we were wearing, we headed south.

Branch: You got ready in one day?

Gentry: Well, yes. In one day. We took off and went to Florida.

Branch: They just drove through and…

Gentry: As I said, they had written a letter to me. I knew about them, but we didn't know whether they were actually coming through Columbus or not. During that time, the black coaches from the black schools in the South used to come up North. But let me first explain this to you: You see, at that time, there was great tokenism in the Big Ten. Well, not only in the Big Ten, but in the North, period! You would find one or two black athletes in every school. Ohio State had its Bill Bell and its Charlie Anderson. And then later on its Bill—oh, I can't think of his last name. It'll come to me later. Well, they all had them—all had one or two blacks. However, they did not want a whole lot of blacks because, as I said before, when they played teams in the South, they couldn't take their black athletes with them. That meant Maryland, Virginia, let alone Tennessee, Georgia, Alabama and all the border states. When they went across the Mason-Dixon Line, Bill Bell, and other athletes like him, were not able to play with the team. So, they didn't want a lot of blacks because, you see, they would mess up their team when they would go South. When they traveled, they needed to have a full team. So if they had only one or two blacks on the team, they could be left at home and they would still have opportunity for a full team to travel.

Alright. Consequently, there were numerous black athletes in the Northern area, especially in Ohio, Pennsylvania and places like that. So these noteworthy black athletes would graduate from high school and would have no place to go. The Northern schools could not absorb all of them—just as I was turned down at OSU because they already had their quota of blacks.

Branch: So you are saying that you had to go from the North to the South?

Gentry: Yes, I am saying that we went with the black coaches who would come from the South to the North to recruit us. I remember Alabama State used to bring their bus. Incidentally, they had offered me a scholarship. They would go all through the North and return to the South with a bus-load of athletes. All of these unclaimed athletes were up there, and the black coaches from the South would come up North and get a bunch of them. When I went to FAMU in 1939, there were, I would say, only about nine or ten players on the team out of Florida. The rest of them were from the northern tier. Remember, it was Bill Bell and Jake Gaither who picked me up from the North and took me South to school.

Branch: Do you think that maybe your grades could have had something to do with your having been rejected by OSU?

Gentry: No. I had enough grades. Since the "Dumb Room" experience, I had, by the time of graduation from high school, acquired enough grades to get into college. But let me tell you this. For in-state students, there was an open door policy, more or less. And being an outstanding athlete, if it were a matter of academic deficiencies, I would have gotten into OSU. Because, then, as now, a way is found to get athletes into school.

Branch: Do you regret not having gone there?

Gentry: Now, as I look back, let me tell you. When I used to go out on the road recruiting, trying to encourage the Northern boys to come to my school down here at TSU, one of the things that I would point out to them was this: I would point out to them the number of black athletes who actually graduated from college at those schools. Now, you check the records—from Bill Bell in the early 30s. You can take one hand and you can count all the black football players that graduated from OSU, and I believe you can cut off some of your fingers. As sure as I am sitting here, I would have never graduated from Ohio State University.

Branch: Why? Do you think that you would not have gotten the push that you needed or equal treatment?

Gentry: I would have been like all the rest of the guys. Like Charlie Anderson and many of the other blacks that went there, I don't believe that I would have passed. I don't believe that they would have shown enough concern to actually... I believe I would have played football there. And I believe I would have stayed there for four years, but I don't believe that I would have graduated. No more than Jesse Owens. Jesse Owens did not graduate from OSU. And, even today, as we think about it, we can only surmise the reasons why black athletes were not graduating.

For Howard Gentry, Sr., athletics opened the doors to success and a sound education.

All-City
High

Tackle Howard Gentry

Basketball

Track

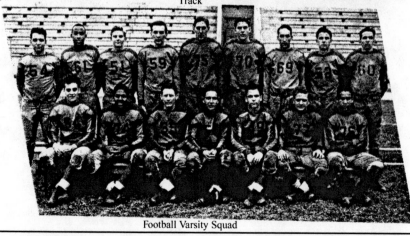

Football Varsity Squad

The Columbus Dispatch
Wednesday
JANUARY 29, 1992

Accent

Athletics not always an open field

Howard Gentry's plight reflected obstacles faced by area blacks

Stories by Bob Hunter
Dispatch Sports Reporter

When he was growing up on the Hilltop in Columbus in the 1930s, Howard Gentry's boyhood heroes wore scarlet-and-gray uniforms and leather helmets.

They were white. He was black.

He didn't think it mattered.

"I wanted to go to Ohio State more than anything in the world," Gentry said. "It had always been a dream of mine to play there from the time I was little, and I gave it everything I had."

Gentry loved Ohio State football so much, he joined the Boy Scouts so he could sell programs at OSU home games on Saturdays. He played enough football when he wasn't hawking lineups to become an all-city player at West High School in 1937 and 1938.

In the pristine days before recruiting coordinators, recruiting "experts" and radio talk shows, those honors should have been the answer to his boyhood dreams.

But Gentry, a talented football player, a good student and a model citizen, had everything going for him except the thing that mattered most: skin tone.

"Some Ohio State alumni who were black took me up there, and the athletic director (Lynn St. John) refused to talk to me," he said. "The head coach (Francis Schmidt) refused to talk to me. Ernie Godfrey, the freshman coach, finally told me that they had all the blacks they could handle at the time and that they weren't very good students. He said I was wasting my time."

The early history of black athletes in Columbus involves a lot of wasted time.

Black baseball players formed teams because they couldn't hope to play on white teams. Black football players did likewise.

Homer Tyler formed a semipro black all-star football squad as early as 1904, knowing its opponents would be teams similar to his or black college teams such as Wilberforce.

Although there were isolated cases of racial

Gentry today

Gentry as a standout football player at West High School in 1937-38

J. Higgins, far left, played with a white Columbus baseball team in 1887.

Columbus Metropolitan Library

equality — Frederick D. Patterson became the first black to play on the Buckeye football team in 1891; Julius B. Tyler followed in 1896 and even scored a touchdown — they were hardly the norm before the 1940s.

Patterson, so light-skinned that he doesn't stand out among his white teammates in an 1891 photo, was the son of a prominent Greenfield, Ohio, businessman who owned C.R. Patterson and Sons, carriage manufacturers.

Tyler belonged to a successful Columbus family; his brother, Ralph Waldo Tyler, was a prominent journalist who was *Dispatch* society editor for 30 years and who was sent by Publisher Robert Wolfe to cover the 1908 Republican National Convention, which nominated William Howard Taft for president.

Extensive research by Hiram L. Tanner, retired reporter for the *Columbus Call and Post*, shows that, after Tyler, OSU didn't field another black football player until 1929, when Bill Bell joined Sam Willaman's squad.

Unfortunately, controversy followed Bell. When OSU played Navy in Baltimore on Nov. 8, 1930, word spread that Bell wouldn't make the trip. The reason? Northern schools didn't use blacks in visits to "Southern" schools, and OSU officials determined that Bell should not visit Baltimore.

"At the time, a big fuss was made over it," Tanner said. "A lot of people blamed Willaman, but it was later shown that the school president, Dr. (George) Rightmire, made the decision.

"Willaman actually deserves a lot of credit for helping open things up to black football players. Besides Bell, he also had another black, Russell Embrey, on his team in 1930, but he had to leave because of academic trouble."

Basketball had its troubles, too. In 1930, Wilbur Meade, an all-state

Please see GENTRY Page 2E

The road to equality was long and winding

He stares into the 1990s from a faded 1887 photograph, a black man on an otherwise white baseball team. His last name is Higgins. Today, baseball researchers know his first name only as J.

J. Higgins was the first black man to represent Columbus in the then-white world of professional sports.

And he was the last to share a dugout with the city's white professionals until pitchers Brooks Lawrence and Bill Greason were sent to the Columbus Redbirds by the St. Louis Cardinals in 1954, seven years after Jackie Robinson broke the color line in the major leagues.

By then the novelty of loudmouthed fans mercilessly riding black players had worn off somewhat, at least in the North.

"We really didn't have any problems," Lawrence said. "They wanted a winning ballclub, and we helped them win. The guys and the fans here (in Ohio) were fairly decent. But then I had played at Portsmouth, Va., the year before, which is all I think I really need to say about that."

Lawrence spent seven years in the major leagues, five with Cincinnati, and didn't look back. Today he coaches baseball at Wilmington College in Ohio.

Greason, whose minor-league exploits logged him only three weeks in the majors that summer, had a different experience, mostly because of his background.

Lawrence had grown up in Springfield, Ohio, and commuted between his home and Redbird Stadium until he was called up by the Cardinals in June.

Greason grew up in Atlanta, so he lived in Columbus for all but the three weeks in St. Louis that summer.

"After we played the game, my teammates went

Please see EQUALITY Page 2E

GENTRY from 1E

player from Hamilton, Ohio, enrolled at OSU and tried out for basketball. Harold G. Olsen, the Buckeyes' coach from 1923 to 1946, pulled aside his young assistant coach, Floyd Stahl, and told him to take care of the situation.

Sixty-one years later, Stahl remembers how it shook him.

"Oly called me over and told me to tell him that he would be better off if he went someplace else," said Stahl, who had coached at Dayton Stivers High School the year before.

"I just felt terrible. I said, 'Do I have to?' He said, 'Yes. It will be better for him if he goes somewhere else. He won't be able to stay with us when we play away from home; he won't be able to eat with us; there'll be all kinds of problems.' "

Meade transferred to Oberlin (Ohio) College, but the issue arose again in 1935, when James Wood, chosen as a high school All-American in basketball by a Chicago publication, enrolled at OSU. Wood had been a star at Louisville (Ky.) Central High School and had a scholarship offer from Kentucky State, but he chose OSU.

He played on the freshman teams in football and basketball but won his numeral only in basketball.

"He asked Dick Larkins, the coach of the freshman football team, why he didn't get his numeral in football," said Wood's brother, Mirt. "And Larkins (who later became OSU athletic director) said, 'I can't tell you. I really don't know why he didn't get one. I can't understand it myself.' "

So Wood gave up on football in 1936 and concentrated on basketball, his best sport. But again he reached a dead end.

"He went out for the team," Mirt Wood said, "but after a couple days of practice he was told not to come out anymore. They couldn't truthfully cut him, but that's what they did. The other players knew it wasn't right, but there was nothing they could do.

"My brother was really bitter about it. It didn't ruin his life or anything, but it really upset him. He quit school not long after that and played pro basketball in Philadelphia for a while and eventually came back and finished school. But he never forgot that. He knew he was good enough to play and didn't get to. It always bothered him."

If Wood had been a track star, he probably wouldn't have had a problem.

By the time Jesse Owens, David

Cleo "Chico" Vaughn began playing for Ohio State in 1954.

Albritton and Melvin Walker rose to prominence at Ohio State in the 1930s, the OSU track team had featured numerous black stars, starting with Dan Ferguson in 1911.

"It was an unwritten law in the Big Ten that blacks wouldn't be allowed to play in basketball," Tanner said. "But in track, you couldn't keep them down. If somebody can outrun your best athletes, you have to let him on the team."

Not so in basketball. The OSU team wouldn't see another black until 1954, when Stahl, then head coach, lured Cleo "Chico" Vaughn from Lima, Ohio.

Again the story ended unhappily. Vaughn played a year of freshman ball and a year of varsity, then quit the team because of the pressure.

"It was like a miniature Jackie Robinson thing," said Vaughn, who has changed his name to Chico and today runs basketball camps for inner-city youths in Toledo. "We went to Louisville, and we went to Miami, Fla., and there were a lot of jeers, a lot of people calling me 'nigger,' stuff like that.

"I had to stay in the Venetian Hotel in Miami for seven days and could not leave my room because of the way things were."

In Columbus, Vaughn said, he was treated like a celebrity, which featured more downs than ups.

"A lot of people didn't understand what I went through," he said. "If I scored 11 points, that wasn't enough. If I missed four of five shots, everyone wanted to know why. People thought, because I was black, I was supposed to score a lot of points, but we had Paul Ebert, a two-time All-American, and Robin Freeman on that team, and that (scoring) wasn't my role.

"I had too much to live up to. I was the wonder boy. One game I even stayed at home in my apartment. After two years, I couldn't take it anymore."

By the 1950s, OSU football had opened to blacks, mostly because of Paul Brown. Brown succeeded Schmidt as coach in 1941 and welcomed Bill Willis, an East High graduate who was bound for Illinois. Willis was the only black on the

squad that year, but by his senior year, 1944, several blacks were on the Buckeye roster, Willis said.

He wasn't allowed to live on campus, he said, but Brown always treated him fairly. Brown had been the reason he chose OSU over Illinois, Willis said.

"My high school coach, Ralph Webster, had contacted the athletic director and coach at Illinois, and it was all set for me to go there," he said. "But because of Paul's reputation, Webster told me that I'd be better off going to Ohio State, and he was right.

"Paul made a difference. There were only two or three other blacks in the whole league at the time, but I hardly noticed. Paul treated me the same as everyone else, and by the time I left there were several blacks on the roster.

"Later, when I played for him when he had the Browns in the All-American Conference, he was the first to use blacks in that league. I think he surprised a lot of people."

Gentry, the West High senior who had found OSU's doors closed only a few years before, also surprised a few people. After bitterly saying he wouldn't go to college and accepting a job as a doorman at the Deshler-Wallick Hotel in Downtown Columbus, Gentry took a verbal beating from older brother Harry, who refused to let him waste his talent.

After achieving black All-American status at Florida A&M, Howard Gentry became a highly successful football coach at Tennessee State in Nashville, was promoted to athletic director and eventually sat on the prestigious NCAA Council for three years.

Today, at 70, Gentry is retired and living in Nashville, home of the 10,000-seat Howard C. Gentry Athletic Complex, which includes an Olympic-size swimming pool and a 200-meter track. The school recently established a scholarship in his name.

"I've always wondered what would have happened to me if my brother hadn't forced me to go to college," Gentry said. "I was the most disappointed person in the world when I found out that Ohio State didn't have a place for me, and I really didn't have any desire to go anywhere after that happened.

"If it wasn't for Harry, who knows what might have happened to me, all because Ohio State wouldn't take me. I think about it all the time. It's kind of scary."

West High School

ATHLETIC DEPARTMENT
COLUMBUS, OHIO
OTTO H. MAGLY, Principal

ATHLETIC COMMITTEE
J. C. BELTZ
C. A. KENNEDY
C. B. MARQUAND
C. W. MICHEL
O. C. MONTGOMERY

ATHLETIC DIRECTOR
HAROLD E. WISE

COACHES
HAROLD E. WISE — Football,
Basketball, Baseball
GEORGE G. COLLINS — Track,
Minor Sports, Ass't Football and Basketball

Howard Gentry:

The Athletic Committee of West High School wishes to congratulate you as a member of the city championship football squad of 1936. Your spirit of unselfishness, willingness to work and fine sportsmanship did much to make possible the very successful season which we have just closed.

We desire on behalf of the Athletic Committee of West High School, the student body and faculty to assure you of our appreciation.

C. W. Michel

Columbus O 11-11-38

Dear Howard,

So very sorry you were not on a winning team this year, but I am proud of you for the fine work you did for the team, and I am sure the critics will bestow honorable mention of your ability, which in my humble opinion, you so justly deserve.

In conclusion Howard keep up the good work, be honest, be industrious, and be above all a gentleman, learn to control yourself, which helps one to control others.

With best wishes for you success, I am,

Most Sincerely
Edgar Birkhead

CHAPTER FIVE

College Years

"When I went down to Florida, you know, I knew that I would make the ball club down there, and I knew that I would be a star just like I was in high school. But I had the rudest awakening that I had ever had." — *Howard C. Gentry, Sr.*

Gentry and Branch continued the interview by discussing the college years.

Branch: Do you regret not having gone to OSU?

Gentry: Now let me tell you. The best thing that ever happened to me was that they refused me! Because when I went to FAMU—but let me give you another little story here—when I went to FAMU, I was a cocky youngster.

Branch: You're still a cocky, grown-up youngster!

Gentry: Well, OK. But when I went down to Florida, you know, I knew that I would make the ball club down there, and I knew that I would be a star just like I was in high school. But I had the rudest awakening that I had ever had. When I got down there, I found that I was used as a cannonball. Some of the greatest football players that I have ever come into contact were at Florida A&M University.

Branch: Who were some of them?

Gentry: Now, there was a guy by the name of Stanley Strong. He could have played football for anybody in the United States. He could have made a tremendous professional fullback. There was Hank Butler. Incidentally, Hank Butler was from Columbus, Ohio. He was a great halfback. He could have played at Ohio State. He could have played at any Big Ten school. He was an All-American (black). Neely was from Columbus, Ohio. Murray Neely was a tackle. He was great. Gant was from Sandersky, Ohio. See, all of these boys were from Ohio. His brother, however, was one of the tokens at Cincinnati. But Roy Gant ended up at FAMU. He was, by far, one of the most versatile football players that I have ever seen in my life. He made All-American at guard; he made All-American at end. He could have made All-American in any position he played. This was the caliber of young man who was at FAMU—the kind who are now at the Big Ten schools. These boys were down at the places like FAMU, Alabama State, and the like.

Now, as I was saying, I went down there, and I found that I was not that great at all. But, incidentally, I have the distinction of being the only letter winner in the freshman year in college at FAMU. But the reason that I lettered was because everybody got hurt, and they had to play me. I have a book here now that tells about me making the team and earning a letter my freshman year. But I did not deserve to be on that team because I was not good enough!

Branch: Jake Gaither was the coach?

Gentry: Jake Gaither was the assistant coach. Bill Bell was the Head Coach. Now, let me tell you something academically about Bill Bell. William Bell was a student. He graduated from Ohio State University. He got his masters degree from OSU, and he later got his doctorate from OSU. Incidentally, he has gone into the OSU Hall of Fame. He was inducted about four or five years ago. He was a real gentleman! Thank God during my whole experience, I came up under great coaches, and Bill Bell and Jake Gaither were two of them!

They didn't have big staffs in black colleges at that time, but at FAMU there was another coach by the name of Horace Bell. He was Bill Bell's brother. He was a great football player who had played on the All-Star team for Minnesota. So, the coaching staff was made up of Bill Bell, the Head Coach, Jake Gaither, the backfield coach, and Horace Bell, the line coach.

At this point, I would like to tell you of some things that occurred during my freshman year at FAMU. They are important happenings for I know that they had an impact upon the rest of my life.

During my freshman year as I told you, I had been used as a cannonball and, incidentally, these guys had just won the black National Championship the year before. So, they didn't really need me, and they just pushed me around. Oh boy it was tough. It was hot down there, and the only reason that I didn't go home was because I just did not have the money, so I stuck it out. And I am so happy that I did!

To this day, I still don't know why I did this. But one day they had me down there and they were knocking me around. It was hot and I was not used to that heat. And something happened to me and the line coach Horace Bell said something to me, and I jumped up and said, "Hell! Don't holler at me when I'm hot!" Can you imagine saying the word "hell"? Well, that meant that I had to leave the field. So I left the field and went to my room. That night, Jake Gaither, along with Coach Bell, came to my room. They told me that I was not using the proper language, and that they could not tolerate that kind of language, and that as far as my performance was concerned, I was not doing well there. And they told me, point blank, that the next time that anything like that happened, I would be sent away from that school. That was the kind of treatment that I got, and it certainly did not boost my ego.

Branch: What were your grades like at that time?

Gentry: As far as my academic progress was concerned, I guess I had a D+ average at the end of my freshman year. My sophomore year I took a course in general psychology, and I flunked that course and I never shall forget the result of it.

Branch: What happened?

Gentry: The fact is that we used to have to go by bus on all of our athletic trips. We would travel all day from Sunday morning and not get back to the campus until Sunday night. Well, Monday morning I did not feel like going to class, and many times I did not go. I never shall forget the lady who taught the psychology class. Her name was Dr. Catora Whitehurst. At the end of the course, she said this to me, "Mr. Gentry, if you come to my final examination and make an A, I am still going to flunk you. You didn't come to my class." So, I didn't take the examination for I knew that I was going to get an F. Now as a result of that and my D+ average to begin with, it put me on probation—academic probation.

Now this is the most wonderful thing that happened in my life. The dean of the college, Dean Southall, sent me a letter informing me that I had been placed on academic probation, and a copy of that letter was sent to the coach. Jake Gaither called me to the office, and he picked up the letter and he said, "I see you are on academic probation. I want you to know that I am not depending on you next year."

Even though I was not doing well in my classwork, I just knew that I was going to be a first stringer the next year because a lot of the guys were graduating, and because of the prior injuries, I had already gotten a chance to play. Even so, he told me that he was not depending on me.

By that time, however, I had resigned myself to being in college there, and I did not want my bubble to completely burst. I said to myself, "You mean to tell me that I will be sent home because of poor academic standing!" My brother Joe had graduated from Bluefield. Two of my sisters were still in college. Another of my sisters was teaching. Now this became sort of traumatic for me. I knew that I wanted to play football, and I knew that I did not want the embarrassment of being sent home. Of significance is the fact that the coach did not promise me that he would see to it that a tutor would be provided for me. He didn't promise me anything! He just said that he was not depending on me the next year. I didn't have any books, and they did not give you books at that time. I had a work-aid job, and I found me some books. And I want you to know that the next semester, I made all passing marks, and I came off scholastic probation at the end of that semester. And absolutely, without a doubt, these occurrences—unacceptable language, flunking courses, probation, and most importantly, the reactions of that teacher and the coaches—caused me to rethink my purpose and my desire for my life. It was during that period that I seriously became a student, not just an athlete. I stayed in school and I can truthfully say that the subsequent experiences and achievements while there were the beginnings of my preparation for acquiring whatever I have achieved in life.

Branch: Did you subsequently share these experiences with your students and others?

Gentry: I have told this to my students and others every place that I have worked. And I, too, like my former teacher and coaches, have been very rigid and have made it mandatory that academics preceded participation. I saw to it! As an example, look upon this wall where we are standing. That is a framed poster of my Tennessee State University 1956 Championship Football Team. And, incidentally, my wife made it and gave it to me for one of our anniversaries. In the shape of a football, the poster is made up of a picture and name of each of the young men appearing on that championship team. All but two of them graduated from college. Yes, that is my 1956 Championship Team—the black Championship Team. They were undefeated champions. They played their post-season game against my old alma mater FAMU in the Orange Blossom Classic in Miami, Florida. The coach of that team was none other than one of my old coaches who had become the well-known Head Coach of the FAMU Rattles—Jake Gaither!

We won the game by just two points, and in the midst of our jubilation, I could still hear and can still recall Coach Gaither saying that since he had to lose the game, he was glad that the loss was to one of his boys.

But getting back to what these guys whose pictures are on the poster are doing in life: I can tell you where they all are and what they are doing. This one, to which I am pointing, has his own management firm now. He was the top man in the Department of Health and Welfare in the District of Columbia before he went into his own business. Prior to that, he was with HEW, and he headed up the southwest region. That guy is going to do great things the rest of his life. As I point to this one, he is a teacher in Port Arthur, Texas. This young man is a teacher in Chattanooga, Tennessee. This one has his Ph.D. He is in Orlando, Florida. This one is teaching in Orlando, Florida. This one is in Atlanta, Georgia. This one has a security business in Los Angeles. This one has a travel agency in Memphis, Tennessee. This one is a principal in Louisville, Kentucky. This one played with the Denver Broncos and is now a probation officer in Denver, Colorado and also has a business there. This one is a football coach in Chicago, Illinois. This one was teaching in Memphis, but now has a fleet of tractor trailers.

Branch: Let me interrupt you and ask you—how did you get into coaching in the first place?

Gentry: OK. Well to get back—you know, I get to talking about these guys, and I'm just so proud of them, and as I point to members of that group, we've also got medical doctors, we've got Ph.D.s, we've got dentists and business men. And I'm so proud to talk about them. But, what did you ask me?

Branch: How did you get into coaching?

Gentry: Now, how did I get into coaching? OK. We always come back to this Bill Bell from Ohio State University. Now, I became a student and before I left Florida A&M my senior year, I was an All-Conference Tackle, and I also made the Chicago Defender All-American Team that year. My telling you about this and my connection with Bill Bell while at college and my subsequent military experience will help me to adequately answer that question.

1961

1939

Front row: (left to right) Coach A. S. Gaither, Eddie Sherfield, Leo Harrison, Charles Edwards, Edward Oglesby, Howard Gentry, Oswald Glymph, William Horton, Glenn Dowdell, James Wanza, Macon Williams, Thomas Sutton, William Simmons, Dean J. B. Bragg, Coach William Bell. *Second row:* Coach Horace Bell, Allen Killens, Obia Jennings, Earl Jones, Thomas C. Jones, Robert Mike, James Smith, Emerson Cabell, James Gardener, Edward Gilliam, Nicholas Williams, George Tillman. *Third row:* Henry Dixon, John Monroe, Donald Noble, Beverly Scott, James Hawkins, Hansel Tookes, Harold Jones, Richard Harrison, Andrew Simms, William Garnes. *Fourth row:* James Drayton, Israel Payton, Reche Simms, Albert Gant, George McDuffie, Sammie Gardener, Barney Holloman, Clarence Mitchell, James Grant, Leon Watts, Joseph Jackson. *Fifth row:* Guy Pete, Grover Crumsby, Warren Carter, Nathaniel Greene, Wilford Anderson.

CHAPTER SIX
Military Years

"They had assigned me to an all-white officers' cadre by mistake! He left me stand-ing there, went out, jumped in his jeep, and went to the battalion to see whether or not he could get rid of me because they had made a mistake on the assignment of a black into a white cadre—an officers' cadre." — *Howard C. Gentry, Sr.*

G entry: About three or four weeks prior to my graduation from college—I'm going out with my class now—I had enlisted in the reserves, the Enlisted Reserve Corps. Now I did that to stay out of the army! But they called in all reservists, and I was called in three weeks before graduation. I had to go to Fort Hayes in Columbus, Ohio for induction. And, incidentally, the college, because I was so close to graduation—only three weeks away from completion—granted my degree from Florida A&M University. That was a good thing for me because some of my buddies, who had several months to complete this work, had to go back after their tour of duty.

Branch: Did you stay at Fort Hayes for your basic training?

Gentry: No, they sent me to Camp Lee, Virginia, right outside of Petersburg, Virginia—the Quartermaster Corps. When I went there, I found a lot of my buddies coming from black colleges and universities all over the country. And, incidentally, many of them were athletes, specifically foot-ball. So, we went there, and they sent us through basic training and after that, technical training. Then they sent most of us to administrations and supply school. We made such high grades until they thought that we were cheating on the examination. They had never seen a group from black col-leges, so that was something!

Branch: What was that year?

Gentry: That was 1943. So, after that, they put us in cadre school. They made non-commissioned officers out of us.

Now, let me tell you what happened. Camp Lee, Virginia, like many other army posts of that type, had a football team. Never before, however, had they had any blacks on their team, but the call was made—and they had black regiments and they had white regiments—and when the call was made, I went out for the team, as well as a couple more of the other black guys. Well, we caused a problem. Even though they had guys who were there from Ohio State, Alabama, Notre Dame, the Pros, and every place else, we went out there to make the team. I went out there to make the team, and I made the team. Well, then they had another problem. They couldn't get a schedule.

Branch: Because of the black players?

Gentry: Yes, because of the black ball players. They called us in one day and said, "Well, we won't be able to have a team because we cannot get a schedule. But if we can get a schedule, we will call you back." Well, I knew exactly what was happening there, and they sent me on back to my black regiment.

But, in a few weeks, about two weeks later, they called me to come back. And they had a schedule. Our first game was going to be with the Brooklyn Dodgers football team. You remember the old Brooklyn Dodgers professional football team? And the next game was with the New York Giants. Well, this was right up my alley. It was the thrill of a lifetime!

I played football at Camp Lee for three years. Now how did I do that? The first year that I went out for the team I played. And after that year was over, I was able to go to Officer Candidate School at Camp Lee. And while I was in Officer Candidate School, they would take me out of the ranks every day to go to football practice. So, I played football while I was in OCS. Immediately, after I graduated from OCS, they sent me overseas. I met my outfit at the Battle of the Bulge area. Thank God that was over at that time. That's where I found my outfit—35 Quartermaster Truck Company Heavy. That's where I found my group. Now, that's another story in itself. But let me go on to the football. No, I have to tell you this first because it was a meaningful happening in my life.

When I reported to my outfit, we were with the first army, and when I finally found them, I went into the orderly tent. They were out in the field when I reported. The captain was white and I reported, "Lieutenant Gentry reporting for duty, sir." This gentleman looked up and said, "What?!" He left me standing there in the orderly tent. They had assigned me to an all-white officers' cadre by mistake! He left me standing there, went out, jumped in his jeep, and went to the battalion to see whether or not he could get rid of me because they had made a mistake on the assignment of a black into a white cadre—an officers' cadre. This he was not immediately able to accomplish.

Branch: What happened then?

Gentry: They had to keep me, but I want you to know that to be out there following the first army was a tough situation. I had been assigned to a transportation corps-type activity, and I'd had no experience in convoy operation. I'd had one course in convoy operation and that's all. But I knew that having been an enlisted man, I knew that all I had to do was to follow the directions of the individuals who knew the job. Those were the enlisted men!

Branch: The white individuals?

Gentry: They were black. All the enlisted personnel were black. All the officers were white. That's why they wanted to get rid of me. Now, in that they could not get rid of me, they ostracized me. When I would come into the company tent to eat, they would get up and leave. When it was time for sleeping, I would have to go someplace by myself and sleep. The only contact I had was with the black enlisted personnel.

Branch: Were you bitter about that?

Gentry: No. It was a wonderful experience. It made me grow, and they grew. I want you to know that after six months, the orders came through to get me out of that company but by that time I was performing all of the First Officer's duties and responsibilities—I was the INE officer; I was the V.D. officer. I was doing everything. They were depending on this black, and they would no longer segregate me. It was a learning experience for them as well as a learning experience for me.

So, when the orders came for me to leave and go with 3494 QM Truck Company Heavy, this same captain who initially left me standing, begged me not to leave. But the 3494 was shipped through the United States to the South Pacific area. It was a chance for me to come back. I would have been a fool not to take it. So I said no. And I took the chance to come back to the U.S. After I got back to the U.S., they sent me right back to Camp Lee, Virginia. And what did I end up doing when I got back to Camp Lee, Virginia?

Branch: Coaching football?

Gentry: No. It was just about time for the season to start, so I went back to playing football. That was my third year. So, three years in the army, I played football during each of those years. Now I'm still trying to get to how I got into coaching.

Branch: When did you decide that you wanted to be a coach?

Gentry: OK. Now, let me tell you. I was a Health and Physical Education major. Football was my life then. I loved it. My senior year in college, Jake Gaither had to have surgery for the removal of a tumor on the brain. They were short of personnel. They never had but three coaches. So what they did when they had the coaches meeting and when they worked on the program for the day, they would call me in and I would sit and they would give me a slip as to the program that the line would go through that day. So I became a playing student/assistant coach.

Now, Bill Bell went into the military. He went into the Air Force. He went to Tuskegee, and he coached the famous Warhawks. There he heard about my playing for Camp Lee. When he got ready to be discharged, he got an offer to coach at North Carolina Agricultural and Technical College (A&T College) in Greensboro, and he decided that he wanted me as a member of his staff. So, he wrote to me. Soon after getting his letter, the Warhawks were playing a game in Washington, D.C. Excitedly, I went up to see him, and he told me that if I could get out of the army that I had a job.

I had a very good friend who was an officer in charge of special services and I went to him, and I told him that I had a chance to get a job if I could get out. And he said, "Howard, I will do everything I can." The next thing I knew, I had my discharge from the army. Since there was a period of time before football season would start, I went home and guess what I did? I enrolled in Ohio State University on the GI Bill to pursue a masters degree in Health and Physical Education.

Branch: A dream come true?

Gentry: Well—that was a necessity then. I was no longer mad because I could go to OSU, get me a masters degree, and go off to A&T College in Greensboro, North Carolina to work with my idol, who was then the Head Coach and head of the Department of Health and Physical Education.

1943

CHAPTER SEVEN
A&T College

"Black coaches have been master teachers. Since integration, in most instances, they have gotten not the blue chipper but instead they have taken the so-called second best and they have made champions of them!" — *Howard C. Gentry, Sr.*

G entry: After completing two quarters toward my master's degree, I was hired, pending the completion of my degree. I was hired as an assistant football coach and teacher of Health and Physical Education. That is how I got my start into coaching.

Of note, at this time also, is the fact that after I arrived there, I was told that I was also to be the Head Coach of the baseball team! That was the shock of my life, for I knew very little about the techniques and rules of that sport. Nevertheless, I was encouraged to just go and talk with some of the old players on the team. And also I was told to go and talk with some of the guys sitting around the barbershop because they were said to talk baseball all the time. This I did, and of all things, our baseball team won the CIAA—Central Intercollegiate Athletic Association—conference championship that year!

Branch: Let me ask you this: You finally got back to OSU. You are on your way to becoming a very successful coach. Let's talk about the differences you saw then and maybe the differences you see now in the facilities and the programs in predominately white OSU and other predominately white schools and what you had to work with at A&T.

Gentry: First, let me tell you this: When I left high school in Columbus, Ohio and went to Florida A&M, I wanted to major in Industrial Education, but the facilities were so meager until I decided to go into physical education.

Branch: Let's do a comparison.

Gentry: The facilities were not as good as they were in my high school. The facilities were the most meager facilities in the world. But let me tell you something. Some of the best students that I have ever seen came out of those kinds of schools. I'm talking about friends that I met there who are now leaders in the medical community, for example. It's really amazing!

Incidentally, we, the Physical Education majors, were required to take some of the same courses—anatomy, kinesiology, physiology—along with the pre-med and nursing students. Even so, they had only one skeleton in the whole science building. We used to steal that skeleton at night and take it down to our room and study. And then slip it back up there before classes started. We did not want those majors in pre-med and students in nursing to out strip us. So we would study all night long.

Branch: Let's come back to Ohio State and A&T.

Gentry: OK. Now let's go to OSU and A&T. When talking about facilities, there is no comparison. They did not even have a gymnasium at A&T.

Branch: If there is no comparison, how do we account for the fact that black athletes coming from places that cannot be compared to white institutions in terms of facilities and maybe in terms of academics, in some cases, succeed and excel in a generally thought to be top-of-the-line organization? You look at the NBA, the NFL.

Gentry: It's not the facilities *per se*. Surely, the facilities are important. But there is one thing that has got to be made clear—the black coach. He is one of the greatest teachers in the world. You notice that all of the black coaches around have been teachers. I am sorry to say that, now, they are hiring black coaches in the black schools who do not have teaching responsibilities.

Branch: Do you think that they should still have that responsibility?

Gentry: Yes. I think that if they can keep their hands in the academic pursuits, they would be even better coaches. However, consider a football field. Whether we have eighty thousand seats or two thousand seats, the size of the field is the same. The goal posts are the same. Now, what the student learns, the teacher teaches him—how to block, how to tackle, how to run, and how to kick the ball through the goal posts. Despite the overall quality of the facilities, the black coaches have been masters at teaching. They have taken—you know the saying—they say that you can't make chicken salad out of chicken manure. But black coaches have made something that is exceptionally palatable. Let me give you an example. The bump and run—it was first taught right here at Tennessee State University. Jim Marcellas, one of the football players from TSU, took the bump and run technique to the Kansas City Chiefs. You haven't seen it written any-place, but it was started at TSU by the coaching staff at TSU and incorporated into professional football. Master teachers! Black coaches have been master teachers. Since integration, in most instances, they have gotten not the blue chipper but instead they have taken the so-called sec-ond best and they have made champions of them!

Branch: Let's take Howard Gentry—volatile, hostile, hardworking, from North Carolina A&T. Let's get him to Tennessee. When did he get here? How did that happen?

Gentry: OK. Well, let me tell you what happened. I got married after my first year at A&T. Incidentally, I was engaged my senior year of college, but it went sour. I did not want to marry before I went into the army, and she married while I was in the army. So I wasn't too happy about that. Therefore, when I went to work at A&T, I wasn't too seriously interested in the ladies. However, don't misunderstand me. I was interested in the girls, but the fact is that I definitely wasn't interested in marriage—so I thought. But I did meet my wife Carrie. She was teaching at A&T. She was a very attractive and personable person, and the next thing I knew, I fell in love with her, and at the end of nine months, we got married.

Branch: OK. So you fall in love and you get married. Then what did you do?

Gentry: We had a wonderful life there at A&T. We met wonderful friends and developed lifelong friendships among them, and we continued being hardworking, diligent, and productive teachers and coaches. But at the end of the year, I went to my head of the department and told him that I thought that I needed to get a raise because I wanted to increase my fam-ily and that my wife may not be working. He, in turn, sent me to the president of the university. He listened to me regarding my reasons for requesting a raise, and I also stated that my work had been of the caliber whereby a merit raise would be very much in order. He then (of all things) suggested to me that if my wife should become pregnant, the request for a raise would be considered at that time.

At the end of the day, I went home, told my wife of that encounter and I told her that I was not going to sign a contract for the next year. I told her that we should resign and go home to Columbus where I would register in school to continue work on my degree and, at the same time, I would apply to go back into the army. A person who had become one of my best friends at A&T was a colonel in charge of the ROTC. He was making a career of the military, and the very comfortable way in which he and his wife were living had a great influence upon causing me to make the decision to apply to go back into the army on the competitive tour of duty. I had my commission of second lieutenant, and I felt that my making a career of it would provide the opportunity for me to make a decent living for my family. Therefore, I applied to return to the army.

So, my wife and I left Greensboro, North Carolina, went home to Columbus, Ohio, and moved in with one of my sisters and her husband. I registered into graduate school while, at the same time, waiting for my orders to come for me to report to the army. While in this process, one day my wife announced that she was pregnant. I said, "Oh my gosh, I had better get a job," since I had not yet heard from the army.

BOARD OF STRATEGY—Ready to try out their grid tactics against the Hampton Pirates at Greensboro, N.C., this weekend are the Agricultural and Technical College Football Coaching Staff from left to right: Raymond Hopson (backfield), Howard C. Gentry (line), Head Coach Bill Bell, and Eldridge F. Williams (backfield).

AGRICULTURAL & TECHNICAL COLLEGE BASEBALL TEAM

1947 C.I.A.A. LEADING TEAM: *Front row*: (*left to right*) Mansy Pullen, David Livingstone, Ralph Mason, Willie Walker, Junior Varsity, Joe Grier, Robert Daniels, Robert Young. *Middle row*: Edward Joyner, Hubert Simmons, Robert D. Jackson, George F. Johnson, Milford F. Moffett, Walter Fowler, Robert Lee Williams, Marvin Graeber, William H. Thompson. *Back row*: Manager Clarence Russell; George Knox, Thomas Priestly, Guy Bass, Wilford Jeffries, Edward Martin, Harold Green, Ervin Ford, David Sims, Coach Howard C. Gentry

1946 Howard Gentry and William Bell, Head Football Coach at A&T College

CHAPTER EIGHT
Wilberforce State College

"I sat there and listened to Dr. Walter Struthers Davis talk about what he envisioned for TSU in the future years. He talked about playing football games before crowds of 50,000." — *Howard C. Gentry, Sr.*

G entry: In the meantime, I learned that they needed an assistant coach at Central State University. At that time it was Wilberforce State College. I got in touch with Gaston "Country" Lewis, who was the Head Football Coach and with Mac Green, who was the Athletics Director and Head of the Department of Health and Physical Education, and they offered me the job. Since I still had not heard from the army, I accepted. I was hired as an instructor in Health and Physical Education and as an assistant football coach. A couple of weeks after arriving on the campus of Wilberforce, my orders came from the army. In the meantime, however, I had signed the contract with Wilberforce, so I chose to stay there and not report to the army.

Branch: How long were you there?

Gentry: Just one year. As it turned out, the year that I went there, in 1948, Wilberforce had a great year. We were undefeated until the last game. I was the Assistant Line Coach that year. It just so happened that one of the schools that we played was Tennessee State University. This game was played in Washington, D.C., and it was known as the Capitol Classic. In 1947, Tennessee State also had a great year. They had won the Black National Championship.

Prior to the Capitol Classic game, during a pre-game social, I heard Coach Kean, the Head Coach from TSU, talking in conversation with Country Lewis. Coach Kean was saying that he needed a line coach, and he simply remarked that he knew that Jim Walker, the Head Line Coach at Wilberforce, was one of the best in the country. Then Country Lewis remarked to Coach Kean that he not only had Jim Walker, but he also had a young buck by the name of Howard Gentry, originally from FAMU. Until this day, I believe Coach Lewis shared that information about me in an effort to keep Coach Kean from trying to steal Jim away.

Later, as it happened, when the game was played, Wilberforce beat TSU by a score of 26 to 7, and it was at this time that I was first brought to the attention of Henry Arthur Kean and subsequently, to W. S. Davis, the president of TSU. They noted with dismay that the Wilberforce line was in complete command up front all during the game. It was obvious to all TSU coaches and others that the Wilberforce line play made the difference in the final outcome of the game.

I was later told that after the game, that very night, Davis and Kean began a move to "get him" [meaning me] as an aid on the TSU coaching staff. As a matter of fact, that night after the game I was approached by the business manager of athletes from TSU who asked me if I would be interested in coming to TSU. Of course, I simply responded with the statement that I was always interested in improving my conditions.

After getting back to our respective campuses and several days later, I got a call from Coach Kean, asking whether or not I would be interested in coming for an interview. I told him yes, but in reality, I did not really want to leave Wilberforce. I was only fifty miles from my hometown of Columbus, Ohio. But nevertheless, after talking it over with my wife and her suggesting that I go and look at it anyway, I did just that.

After getting down to TSU, Coach Kean took me over to see the president of the university, Dr. Walter Struthers Davis. I sat there and listened to this man talk about what he envisioned for TSU in the future years. He talked about playing football games before crowds of 50,000. Now, in those Colored schools, if you had 5,000 in attendance, you had a big crowd! He talked about developing All-Americans, not black All-Americans, but simply All-American athletes. He talked about other things, unbelievable to me, that he wanted to do at TSU. I thought that the man was insane! At that stage in my life, I could not conceive of Colored persons having those kinds of things to happen in their lives. Really, it upset me. I went back home and told my wife that the man was crazy! And I said that I was not interested in going to that school!

Nevertheless, I started getting calls from TSU, asking me would I come and their telling me what they would give me. Consequently, it was so bothersome until I did go and talk with the Athletics Director, the Head Football Coach, and the president of Wilberforce College about the offer from TSU. The president told me that he could not promise me anything at that moment but that he would see what he could do. In addition, he said that I might be considered as a future head coach there at Wilberforce.

All things considered, and despite my previous negative feelings about going to TSU, I had to consider the fact that I was being offered an increase in salary, plus a job for my wife, and an apartment for us to live in on campus.

Branch: You couldn't turn that down, could you?

Gentry: Under any circumstance, it was a difficult decision and those that I worked with at Wilberforce did not make it any easier. With my child Carol having been born and being only about six months old, a group of them came by to talk with me and tried to discourage me from taking my family back to the South. You know, everybody had bad things to say about the South and how it treated Negroes. But I said that it was an opportunity for me and the salary that TSU was offering me would result in my making more than the head of the department at Wilberforce. Consequently, even though reluctantly, I decided that I had better go on and take that opportunity.

1948 ANNUAL NATIONAL CLASSIC TENNESSEE STATE VS WILBERFORCE
WILBERFORCE STATE COLLEGE 1948 FOOTBALL COACHING STAFF: *(left to right)* Coach Al Baker, Coach James "Big Jim" Walker, Coach Gentry, and Head Coach Gaston F. "Country" Lewis

CHAPTER NINE
Tennessee A&I State College

"But it should be known, however, that when I, along with my wife and my six-month-old daughter, came to Nashville and to TSU, the foundation of an athletic empire had already been built." — *Howard C. Gentry, Sr.*

Gentry: I came to Tennessee A&I as the Head Line Coach and teacher of HPE and later as Campus Recreation Director. That was my first beginning at TSU.

Branch: And that was what year?

Gentry: That was the fall of 1949. By that time I had the experience of FAMU as a student, a player, and a coach. I had the experience of working under my old coach at A&T, and I had the experience of Wilberforce State under Country Lewis, the Head Coach, and Jim Walker, the Head Line Coach.

Coach Lewis was a master teacher. I heard him participate on clinics, and talking about a man who could explain his system, he was the best! Basically, I knew line play, but Jim Walker taught me T formation line play. So I felt pretty cocky about what I could do.

Branch: So, you were basically a line coach?

Gentry: Yes, a line coach. So when I came here as Head Line Coach, I tried to change some things and argued for some changes. For example, I never saw any reason for double-teaming a man. In other words, you hit fast and you don't need double-teaming. At Wilberforce, they were single blocking and cross blocking, etc. So, over the objections of some of the other coaches who were present at TSU, when I came there, I convinced Coach Kean that we should incorporate that in our offense. Finally, it was incorporated, especially in the line, since I was in charge of the line. That was really my beginning as being in charge of an area of football here at TSU.

But it should be known, however, that when I, along with my wife and my six-month-old daughter, came to Nashville and to TSU, the foundation of an athletic empire had already been built. This had been accomplished under the administration of Dr. Walter Struthers Davis, who was the president at that time, and Coach Henry Arthur Kean. He was Head Football Coach as well as the Director of Athletics and Head of the Department of Health and Physical Education. Coach Kean, who was affectionately known as "The Fox," was a great coach, highly respected, and I learned a lot from him. During his years as Director of Athletics, Head of the Physical Education Department and Head Football Coach, TSU, at that time, started enjoying a "Golden Era" in athletics. He, along with the wholehearted support of President Davis, built the foundation of an athletic empire, which, over the years, resulted in attracting hundreds of talented athletes, numerous ones who excelled in the national arena as well as in international competition and the Olympics.

Of tremendous importance also is the fact that these two men always emphasized and insisted that there was something that was always to be kept uppermost in the minds of those—coaches and others—responsible to them, and it was this: they insisted that all the athletes should be productive students.

As I further reflect upon the coaches that I worked under, I, of course, remember that, as before stated, Coach Kean was a tremendous coach. He was a mathematician by training. He was shrewd. He was a master at planning—strategically moving things. And Country Lewis—I talked about his knowledge of his system and his excellent ability in explaining it. But Bill Bell—I have never seen anyone teach fundamentals as effectively as he could teach them. Without a doubt, the strategies and lessons taught by all of these men stuck with me over the years, and we at TSU continued to have some very good years. As a matter of fact, from 1949, the year that I went there, through 1956, we had National Championship teams.

Before recording the end of my husband's conversation with Mr. Branch wherein he will speak of the circumstances regarding his advancing to the positions of Interim Head Coach and Head Coach, I want to share this observation of him during his beginning years at TSU. As the years passed at TSU, upon applying that which excellent teachers had taught him, my husband proved to be an effective football coach, a dynamic recreational director, and an exceptional teacher. And, with his impeccable character, he became highly respected as he served under Kean with distinction.

Generally speaking, things went along exceedingly well. He continued his graduate studies at Ohio State University, and in 1951, he finished the master's degree. The next year, our second child Howard, Jr. was born.

The intramural activities engaged a large number of participants, and there was always a great number of spectators as well. As my husband continued to run a highly successful intramural program, he never shirked his responsibilities as a teacher, and it continued to be fascinating to him to coach under The Fox, Henry Arthur Kean.

1949

TENNESSEE A&I STATE UNIVERSITY'S COACHING STAFF

Back row: (left to right) Forrest Strange, Lawrence Simmons, J. C. Coffee. *Front row:* Shannon Little, Head Coach Henry A. Kean and Howard Gentry

TENNESSEE STATE 1948 EDITION OF THE 1947 NATIONAL CHAMPS: *First row: (left to right)* Walter Gillispie, Lafayette Lacey, George Quarles, Fred Bullard, Kendrick Marshall, Russell King, Milton Smith, Alvin Poller, Willie Tanner, Clarence Nails; *Second row:* Samuel Green, George Gilchrist, Raleigh Wynn, Luddie Johnson, John Sanders, William J. Smith, Billy Dixon, John Salters, William Rhodes; *Third row:* Joe Herndon, Willie Evans, John Rhodes, John Sharpe, James Maull, William A. Smith, Glasco Franklin, Robert Tapscott, Marvin Bridges; *Fourth row: (left to right)* George Brown, Willie White, Paul Crum, Zenoch Adams, Clifton Lewis, Jesse Joseph, William Fowlkes, Nathaniel Taylor, Charles Hamilton; *Fifth row:* Conrad Perkins, Alvin Sharpe, Grammison Davis, Carl Carter, Bob Fowlkes, Willie Savage

CHAPTER TEN

Interim Head Football Coach/ Head Football Coach

"So, as usual, when considering important decisions, I talked the situation over with my wife." — Howard C. Gentry, Sr.

Gentry: In 1954, however, at a game we were playing at A&T College, Coach Kean became ill and we, the assistant coaches, carried on with the game while Coach Kean sat on the bench. After that, an interesting thing happened to me. Coach Kean thought that he could come back to coaching, so they did not want any [permanent] changes to take place in the make up of the coaching staff. So, the decision was made to place folded pieces of paper in a hat with one piece having an "X" marked on it. We, the coaches, were to draw from it. The one among us, the assistant coaches, to draw the "X" was to be the chairman of the coaching committee, to run football practice in the spring. I was the first to put my hand in the hat and of all things, I drew the "X." And that automatically made me the chairman of the coaching committee for spring practice.

We had spring practice, but Coach Kean's condition still would not allow him to come out for the fall. Consequently, they concluded that a new coach had to be named. They were going to name Lawrence Simmons as the Head Football Coach. He was on the staff when I came to TSU. However, some problems came up, and it was decided that they should not proceed with the previous plans to name him. Consequently, with their having had the opportunity to observe my capabilities, one day Coach Kean and Dr. Davis called me in and simply told me that they wanted me to be the Interim Head Football Coach.

This was an absolute surprise to me, for I knew of their previous plan to name Simmons as the Head Coach. As a matter of fact, Coach Simmons had asked me to be his first assistant, and I had told him that I would be pleased to be his first assistant. Also, the president and Coach Kean had made plans for me to go to Indiana University to work toward the doctoral degree in Health and Physical Education. With these thoughts in mind and also with my not feeling too comfortable about their changed plans regarding my co-worker, I questioned them as to whether or not I had a choice in the matter. But the fact is that they had already made the decision.

So, as usual, when considering important decisions, I talked the situation over with my wife. In the process, I stated that I was not sure that I wanted to be a head football coach, and she countered by matter-of-factly posing the question, "Why are you in it?" As I thought about that question, I took it to mean just that!

Over the years, however, she has said that as she asked that question, she was really at the same time thinking that since I had the opportunity to go to work on my doctoral degree that I, possibly, should make the decision to do that if I were not certain about wanting to be a head coach. Nevertheless, after taking time to further debate the questions of desiring to become the head football coach or not, I finally said OK.

No matter what the real reason was for my wife's question, over the years, I have taunted her with the fact that because of her question and my subsequent interpretation of it, I have accused her of being the reason for my having to deal with so many headaches during subsequent years. This lighthearted accusation I have made because that first challenging head coach position which I chose to take led to other positions which were equally as demanding. The question may arise as to whether I regretted being called upon to serve in those additional positions as well as the head football coach position. My answer has to be absolutely not. I do not regret having served in those head positions. So it was in 1955 that I became the Interim Head Football Coach at TSU, and it was in 1956 that I became the Head Football Coach.

Most people did not know of the terrific pressure I felt upon coming in as Interim Head Coach following Henry Arthur Kean, Sr. He had posted a record of 163 wins, just 34 losses, 5 ties, and three National Championships for his 24 years of coaching. When I took over as Interim Head Coach, his team the previous year had gone undefeated for 10 games and was named co-champions of Negro Collegiate Football for 1954.

On top of following such a noteworthy record, other situations present-ed themselves which were most troubling. First, the very capable Backfield Coach, Lawrence Simmons—the one that was first considered for the head coaching position—left and went to Lincoln Heights High School in East St. Louis, Illinois as Head Football and Baseball Coach. Next, a bad knee sidelined Leon Jamison, the pass-catching sensation who was the receiving half of the Valentine-to-Jamison aerial combination. And, to top off the bad luck situations, before the season started, Fred Valentine, the outstanding quarterback, was benched with a shoulder separation.

Nevertheless, with a great deal of determination and effort, we won our first two games. We slipped past Lincoln 10-7 in the opener, and the sec-ond game, we edged Virginia State 12-7. During this time, everybody was putting in his two cents worth, so to speak. But the third and fourth games we lost, and then there were not too many suggestions but there existed quite a bit of apprehension among some of the coaches as well as among many of the spectators.

So, during the next week's practice after suffering the game losses and with the previous loss of key players, I realized that attempts to execute the same system as before, more than likely, would not meet with desired suc-cess. Therefore, it was at this time that I decided to change the whole offense. We went into the Shannishy and in doing this, there emerged some other exceptionally talented young men. There were Bob Crawford, a quar-terback, Jessie Wilburn and Percy Hines, halfbacks, and William Griffith, a fullback. They were all sophomores, and they, along with their other capable and enthusiastic teammates, propelled us into rolling over our next opponents on the schedule that year with exceptionally high scores. As examples: we beat Paul Quinn [College] by a score of 85-0, Central State of Wilberforce, Ohio, 82-12, and Texas Southern, 38-14. The next year, 1956, our team enjoyed 10 wins, no losses, and no ties, and we became the Black National Champions. And I was selected as Coach of the Year.

After winning all of our games, we became overwhelmed with excite-ment when we were selected to play in the Orange Blossom Classic. This was an annual event whereby a highly rated team was chosen to play against Florida A&M College in the Orange Bowl in Miami, Florida. FAMU was known to always field an exceptional team, and this particular year was no different. They, too, had not lost a game that year.

The excitement and, at the same time, the tension within all of us—the coaches and team, as well as within other contingents (band, fans, administrators)—that followed us to Miami was exhilarating. Topping off the excitement within me, personally, was the fact that FAMU was my alma mater and its coach, Jake Gaither, was one of my old coaches.

We arrived in Miami on Thursday, and attempts were made among all to enjoy the festivities preceding the game which was played on Saturday. But the tension within me just would not go away! Finally, Saturday came. The respective bands, the Florida A&M Marching 100 and the Tennessee State University Aristocrat of Bands, made their appearances on the streets and on to the field of a packed stadium.

My wife, who became Director of the Majorettes that year, tells of there being equal concern among those connected with TSU's band. She says that they were not certain how the spectators would accept their aristocrat style when appearing on the same field with the very popular fast-stepping FAMU Marching Band. Nevertheless, she takes great pride in describing the half-time performance. Her description goes like this:

As Dr. Lula Bartley, the Head of the TSU Health and Physical Education Department, and I were sitting among the crowd in the stadium, we could hear some of them say, "Well, let's see what they are going to do." When it became half-time and time for our band to take the field, we could see the crowd around us sort of settle down and relax as if wishing for our band to hurry on the field, do their show, and get off the field so that the FAMU band could come on out!

Well, lo and behold, and much to their surprise from the sound of the blasting of the first note from the horns and from the first precise stepping of the band led out by the high-stepping Drum Majors and Majorettes, the crowd around us sat up, and we could hear them saying, "Why they are good, too!" Their performance was exceptional, and over the years, they have performed with such style that earned them the title of "Aristocrat of Bands."

Their band director at the time was Frank T. Greer, and he was a great motivator. He continuously preached to the band and to the majorettes that they represented a "Big Picture," not just themselves. He emphasized the fact that whenever and wherever they performed, they must never forget that they were representing Tennessee State University—"The Big Picture!"

As I sit here today and reminisce, I can remember that the game turned out to be an exciting nip and tuck contest and as fate would have it, we came out the winner by a score of 41 to 39. Jake, being the gracious person that he was, told me that if his team had to lose, he was proud that the loss was to one of his boys. To hear him say that caused me to feel a tremendous sense of pride.

There is another voice which I can also clearly remember hearing as we were celebrating after the game. It came from a young student assistant coach who said to me, "Coach, I feel sorry for you." Such a statement in the midst of our jubilation was really a surprise, and I asked him why he was feeling sorry for me. And his answer was simply, "You do not have any place to go but down."

True enough, we had reached the pinnacle in the realm of football accomplishments. And, also, at the same time, we had accomplished the earlier unbelievable aspiration of Dr. Walter Davis, the president of Tennessee State College, concerning his desire for Tennessee State to play games before crowds of forty or fifty thousand spectators. There actually were that many spectators in the stadium!

Even so, the statement made by the young man, though meant to be complimentary on his part, caused somewhat of an eerie feeling within me.

My tenure as Head Coach was only five years, but during that time, the TSU football winning tradition continued. The team won 42 games, lost 10 and tied 1. Also, the team was Midwest Conference champions in 1956, 1959, and 1960. In addition, during this time, the team enjoyed a winning streak of 22 games.

Howard Gentry and Dr. W. S. Davis, A&I
State College President

1956 COACH OF THE YEAR Howard C. Gentry
and James Buford (Captain of Championship
Football Team)

We Salute **The Big Blue 1956 10-0 TSU Football Team** *30th Anniversary*

Assistant Coaches

HOWARD C. GENTRY
Head Coach

HOWARD W. GREEN
End Coach

SAMUEL R. WHITMON
Backfield Coach

J. C. COFFEE
Line Coach

SHANNON D. LITTLE
Defensive Coach and Scout

FORREST W. STRANGE
Center Coach

1956 SEASON'S RECORD

Won 10   Lost 0   Tied 0

own Score		Opp. Score
46	Langston University	7
33	Grambling College	0
45	Prairie View College	6
32	Central State	6
6	Maryland State	0
52	Southern University	6
52	Alcorn A & M College	6
40	Kentucky State College	0
47	Lincoln University	0
41	Florida A & M	39

CHAPTER ELEVEN

Director of Athletics

"While serving as football coach, there existed wonderful friendships and great camaraderie and enjoyment among my husband and the other coaches. However, when he stepped into his new role as Director of Athletics, for whatever reason, some of the previous friendships became questionable and the camaraderie became almost nonexistent." — *Carrie M. Gentry*

As I continue with this story it will be seen that instead of my husband's path leading him downward, quite the contrary took place. It seemed as though each time a high position in his area needed to be filled, he was the one called upon to fill that position. As was the case when there was a need for the hiring of a Director of Athletics.

Homer Wheaton, one of Dr. Davis' longtime confidants, tells that Dr. Davis was always looking for the exceptionally experienced persons to fill positions in all disciplines at Tennessee State University. This, of course, included the field of athletics. Dr. Davis wanted to hire persons who would be effective in their jobs at the university and also be able to interact well with national organizations. He wanted TSU to be propelled into the world arena.

During this time, TSU had some great coaches to come forth, including football coach John A. Merritt; track and field coach, Edward S. Temple; and basketball coach, John McClendon. It is a story in itself about how the institution's second president, Walter S. Davis (1943-1968), succeeded in creating a sports program that was able to compete "in the big time" with white colleges and universities and win national championships. In 1954, Dr. Davis recruited Coach John McClendon, a notable tactician who was accustomed to playing racially integrated teams since 1948 and did not see basketball as black and white. John B. McClendon, who studied at the University of Kansas with the "Inventor of Basketball" James Naismith, joined the TSU staff in 1954. Under Coach McClendon, who invented the fast break as the "Father of Black College Basketball," Tennessee A&I

State University teams became the first to win three consecutive National Association of Intercollegiate Athletics (NAIA) championships: 1956-1957, 1957-1958 and 1958-1959—a record that still stands in American collegiate sports. He left the university in 1959 to coach elsewhere, including professional basketball.

Dr. Davis had hopes that Johnny McClendon, the basketball coach whose teams had won three consecutive National Association of Intercollegiate Athletics Championships and who had also had experience with professional basketball coaching, would come back and take over the administration of the athletic department. After Kean died, McClendon did come back for a short while as a coordinator of Health, Physical Education, Recreation and Athletics. But "Mack" really wanted to get back into coaching, so he left TSU and went to Kentucky State to be a basketball coach.

Wheaton goes on to tell of his being in a discussion with Dr. Davis relative to the athletic directorship vacancy which needed to be filled, and he says that he commented to Dr. Davis, "What about Gentry?" Evidently, that query prompted Dr. Davis to think about the fact that from the time that my husband arrived at TSU, he had performed all of his duties with exceptional skill, expertise and professionalism. At that time, in addition to serving as Head Football Coach, he was effectively carrying out other responsibilities. They included coaching clinics (involving coaches from several Big Ten schools) as well as administrative duties associated with the dominate sport of football.

Consequently, as my husband told me, out of the clear blue sky at a basketball game, Dr. Davis came up to him and asked him if he would consider becoming the Athletics Director. He said that he was taken by surprise and that he told Dr. Davis he would need to think about it because such a move would mean that he would be leaving something in which he was successful and moving into another sphere of activity.

Nevertheless, when he came home, he told me about the offer. He said that he viewed being the Athletics Director as really being the top of the heap in the field of athletics. He further stated that he felt that it would be another tremendous challenge, but he said that he felt that he was ready to take on the challenge. So in the winter of 1961, my husband officially accepted the position of Athletics Director at Tennessee State University.

President Davis was always thinking about what, in the long run, might be best for the university. Therefore, he insisted that the new Athletics

Director get involved in all of the national athletic organizations. With this thought in mind, he arranged for my husband to go to Kentucky and to spend a week with the commissioner of the Midwest Athletic Association. He knew that this person possessed, and would share, a wealth of information that would benefit my husband as he directed the various athletic teams at TSU. And he felt that most certainly the experience would be of value in reinforcing the competence and expertise which he felt my husband already possessed. He also knew that it would be of benefit to my husband as he moved ahead and joined such organizations as the National Association of Collegiate Directors of Athletics (NACDA) and the National Collegiate Athletic Association (NCAA).

While my husband was a football coach, he and the other coaches shared wonderful friendships and great camaraderie. However, when he stepped into his new role as Director of Athletics, for whatever reason, some of the previous friendships became questionable and the camaraderie became almost nonexistent.

This was a great disappointment to my husband, and many times, in our quiet moments, when he would share with me some of his activities and encounters of the day, it was painful for me to listen to him. I could detect sadness in his voice, and I could see the look of unhappiness and dismay on his face. I knew that he had looked forward to continuing the satisfying friendships. And I knew that he missed those relationships, and he missed the enjoyable get-togethers with his co-workers after work.

Amazingly, however, because of his love for the university, and I do believe also that it must have been because of the goodness of God, he was able to go to bed, get up the next day, and go to his job. And each day he did so with an appearance of exuberance, enthusiasm, interest, and without a trace of discontentment or bothersome concern. Every day, for the next 15 years, he presented himself in this way while taking care of responsibilities and while confronting the many difficult challenges that presented themselves.

When he took the job as Athletics Director, he knew that it would not be easy. He knew that it would be challenging. He knew that the job would consist of his coordinating and supervising the total program of athletic activities and events. He knew of the different sports and their coaches, as well as others connected with the program. This included the Athletic Business Manager, the Sports Information Director, the equipment manager, the athletic trainer, and the secretary to the Athletics Director. All of these would come under his supervision. Other responsibilities consisted of such things as banquets, security at events, coaching clinics, recommending capital improvements, bowl games, serving on committees concerning athletics, assisting coaches with their schedules and contracts, eligibility, departmental and conference policies, approving or disapproving of travel and expense vouchers, representing the department on a conference and national level, and approving the overall budgets for athletic teams and the department and other duties as assigned by the president of the university.

Considering the total program under his administration and the persons who would be assigned to carry out specific responsibilities within the program, it was understandable that all—the Athletics Director and others—would not see eye to eye at all times. Frequently, at the end of the day, Tubby would come home and he would sit and talk and talk, attempting to reach proper conclusions regarding some troubling issues of the day. As a matter of fact, he would sort of wear out my ears! But I was thankful that he knew that he could confide in me, and that I would always be there to listen.

Nevertheless, as I recall, there seemed to have existed no job that was too small nor too large for him to tackle and always with the same amount of interest and enthusiasm. Possibly, these qualities about my husband came into Dr. Davis' mind when he decided to offer him the job as Director of Athletics. He may have recalled that when my husband first came to TSU as an assistant coach, he had successfully carried out the responsibility of being in charge of the supervision of the athletes who were housed in the dormitory located next to the president's home.

The athletes lived on the second floor of the men's dormitory, and we lived in an apartment on the first floor. The athletes could get rather noisy and rowdy at times, but my husband's subsequent appearance among them always resulted in causing a respectfully quieting effect. But in addition and unknowingly to the president, he found another way of keeping the noise out of the earshot of the president and his family. This he did by having the noisiest athletes moved into rooms down at the end of the hall, far away from the president's house. Therefore, many times when their loudness would occur it could not be heard by those who might be bothered by it.

Dr. Davis might have also recalled that my husband, while still an assistant football coach, was given the responsibility of making arrangements for the housing and meal arrangements for the football team and other coaches as they traveled to play games in other cities. On the other hand, however, Dr. Davis might have recalled seeing my husband, along with a group of athletes, happily doing the menial job of clearing off a field out in back of the men's dormitory for the purpose of it being used as the practice field for football.

At that particular time, the athletic facilities on the campus of TSU were quite limited. However, if the staff needed to make a way to carry on their program, this they did. But as the years passed during the time my husband served as Athletics Director, there were numerous improvements in the facilities, including the development of a real practice field! Also, in the W. J. Hale Stadium, where the football games were played, the lights were upgraded, seating capacity was increased, a new press box was constructed and new restrooms and dressing rooms were installed. In addition, trainers' rooms, offices and concession stands were built under the seating areas, and an all-weather surface track was built around the football field. And the gigantic sports complex, now known as the Howard C. Gentry Health, Physical Education, Recreation and Convocation Complex, came onto the drawing board.

Intramural Athletics

In 1967, the responsibility for administering and carrying out the functions of intramural athletics at Tennessee Sate University was placed in the Department of Intercollegiate Athletics. Prior to this time, the responsibility for conducting the program of intramural athletics had been in the hands of appointed staff members in the Department of Health, Physical Education and Recreation. However, teaching assignments and the operations of the intramural programs had frequently been a problem resulting in there being a limited program of intramurals. In addition, there existed the glaring fact that outdoor recreational facilities on TSU's campus, except for a swimming pool, were almost nonexistent. In an effort to address these needs, the Facilities Development Council formed a subcommittee to study the problem and to make recommendations toward developing outdoor recreational facilities. The Director of Athletics was appointed chairman of this subcommittee.

With these added responsibilities, my husband proceeded to familiarize himself with like departments at other schools where intramural programs were in place. He found that most of the schools he observed had an administrative organization whereby there was a Director of Intramural Athletics. This person was directly responsible to the Director of Athletics. So, after examining the programs and related pertinent materials at other schools, the Department of Athletics at TSU then proceeded to develop a comparable program. In due time, using knowledge garnered from observations of outdoor facilities at other schools and after studying suitable sites for such on the campus at TSU, numerous multipurpose courts were constructed. These courts were designed to accommodate such activities as basketball, volleyball, tennis, badminton and shuffleboard. Also, special areas were constructed to accommodate such activities as football, soccer, and volleyball.

To further aid in the development of the intramural program, the department was provided with a budget for the purpose of purchasing intramural supplies and equipment. In addition, the department was given the opportunity to hire both a Director of Intramural Athletics and an Intramural Coordinator of Activities for women.

Early in the program, the position of Coordinator of Intramural activities for women was filled, but it took more time to fill the position of director. Nevertheless, the intramural programs for both men and women began right away, and they were carried out in an exceptionally successful manner. Basically, this occurred because the Director of Athletics enthusiastically joined in with the Coordinator of Intramurals for Women, and in addition to his regular duties, took on the added responsibilities of the Director of Intramural Athletics. Even though the program had to be planned and conducted almost simultaneously, there was mass student participation, both as participants on the teams as well as spectators attending the competitive intramural games. Thankfully, before too much more time passed, a Director of Intramural Athletics was hired. This gave the Director of Athletics the opportunity to return to giving 100 percent of his time and attention to his other primary responsibilities—taking care of the administration of the total athletic program. And, while doing this in the exceptional manner in which he pursued all responsibilities that he was called to assume, another request was made of the Department of Athletics.

Governor's Summer Youth Program

During the spring of 1968, the governor of the State of Tennessee, Governor Buford Ellington, requested TSU to prepare a program of recreational activities for youth in the Nashville community. The Department of Athletics was instructed to set up and to operate this program, and it was to be conducted during the summer months. They were instructed to use the teachers and coaches who ordinarily worked with specific activities during the regular school year, along with student assistants who were outstanding in the specific areas helping them, as the directors of the various areas within the program. For example, football coaches and students of football would work with the football; basketball coaches and students of basketball would work with basketball, track coaches and students of track would work with track; and likewise with all the activities included in the program—swimming, gymnastics, dancing, volleyball, and others.

As I write about important things that I personally remember having occurred in my husband's life, I also like to make reference to some of his personal quotations. Upon reviewing one of the many speeches that he was called upon to give, there was a section in one of them where he spoke of this program. He expressed his excitement regarding the formation of this program for the youth of the city. I feel that the content of this quotation tells a great deal about the character of this man and of his desire to inspire youth to be the best that they could be. He said to them:

> My thoughts were how great such a program would be! For
> it is not often that youngsters get the opportunity to be
> taught by and to consult with the best college coaches and
> some of the best performers in the world.

So, again, with a great deal of interest, enthusiasm, and anticipation, the Athletics Director and other staff members proceeded to set up the program on paper and finally presented it to the governor for his consideration. It was thought by him and his staff to be a very good proposal. And almost immediately it was approved and money was made available to put the program into action.

During the summer of 1968, the Governor's program as described was conducted. Tennessee State University was commended for running an excellent program. And it came as no surprise when, on March 14, 1969, the National Collegiate Athletic Association extended TSU a formal invitation to participate in the inauguration of its National Youth Sports Program.

National Youth Sports Program (NYSP)

It is important for it to be known, however, that not only were the sports activities important in the NYSP program, but there were health examinations and follow-ups, nutrition and hygiene instruction, and information concerning career and educational opportunities were also included. With this combination, it was felt that, most certainly, the program would have a lifelong positive impact on the youth. It was believed that there would be the building of good character, the development of an enlightened and motivated spirit, along with an absolute determination to improve ones physical, social, mental and emotional well-being.

Since the time TSU became one of the schools where the National Youth Sports Program was first inaugurated and because of its obvious value, the program has continued to be operated on the campus of TSU as well as on the campuses of many other schools of higher education all over the nation. Even though my husband gave unwavering attention to all responsibilities that he was called upon to assume in the athletic department, the motivational spirit which he displayed among the NYSP attendees was a joy to watch. He would always emphasize to the young girls and boys that they should never forget that they must always live by the NYSP motto which is: "I will walk tall, talk tall, stand tall."

Continuing "Golden Era"

While successfully taking care of the many phases of the program, the Athletics Director never faltered in carrying out the responsibilities associated with providing the needs of the various coaches and their teams. TSU sports continued enjoying a "Golden Era" of progress.

As they engaged in their many contests, the athletic teams participated in local events as well as events of national and international interest. My husband's administration at TSU helped to prolong the national and international recognition of their sports program. Two programs in part stood out in this area, and they were football and track. Appointed to the head coaching position in 1963, John A. Merritt took the football team to national prominence and kept it there for the next 20 years. Merritt, also called "Big John," was a most unlikely prospect for stardom on the national level because of the lack of opportunity afforded him during his high school years. However, he distinguished himself as a person with great drive and tenacity, and so he went on to attend Kentucky State University on a football scholarship and became the coach at Jackson State University in Mississippi. At Jackson State, he compiled an impressive 68-28-3 record and was named Black College Football Coach of the Year in 1962. His record at TSU was even more impressive at 174-33-7. His total win record of 232-64-11 at the time of his death in 1983 ranked him third among other collegiate coaches—behind only Paul "Bear" Bryant of Alabama and Grambling State's Eddie Robinson.

Under Merritt's reign as Head Coach, TSU never had a losing season. In fact, he had four undefeated seasons, while winning six national championships. Merritt sent more than 100 players to the National Football League. Among them were football greats Ed "Too Tall" Jones, Claude Humphrey, Joe Gilliam, Jr., Joe "747" Adams, Brian Ransom, Waymond Bryant, Cleveland Elam, and Nolan Smith. The city of Nashville renamed part of Centennial Boulevard John A. Merritt Boulevard in his honor in 1982. Although Merritt died at the age of 57 on December 15, 1983, he received posthumous acknowledgements for his great coaching record from Congress in February 1984 and was inducted into the College Football Hall of Fame in December 1994 in New York, New York.

The football team was Associated Press and United Press International champions in 1970 and 1973. The team was rated as National Champions by other news media and organizations in 1966, 1970, 1971, and 1973. Also, the team shared the NCAA Mideast Region Championship in 1965 and won the honor outright in 1966 and 1971. It won the Midwest Region Championship in 1972, and in the old Midwest Conference the team won the title in 1961, 1963, 1964, 1965, and 1966. Of further significance is the fact that, at this time, the football team played its first post-season game against an NCAA affiliated school. That game was against Ball State College in the Grantland Rice Bowl. It ended in a 14-14 tie, but since that game and during the period of time that my husband served as Director of Athletics, the Tigers engaged three other teams in the Grantland Rice Bowl and one in the Pioneer Bowl. They won all four scoring TSU 34, Muskingum 7; TSU 26, Southwest Louisiana 25; TSU 26, McNeese State 23; and TSU 29, Drake 7, respectively.

Thus, the TSU footballers had a record in bowl competition of four wins and one tie. And it was during this "Golden Era" that the football team came up with the winning streak of 24 games. The streak began October 31, 1964 and ended with the first game of the 1967 season in a 12-8 loss to San Diego State.

Among other highlights of my husband's administration involving the athletic teams that must not be omitted is the regional telecast of a game with Grambling State University from Hale Stadium on TSU's campus by ABC Television in 1963. This was a first time occurrence, and, of course, one could detect the importance of it in furthering the visibility of TSU nationwide.

Tennessee State University also gained international recognition through the development and excelling of its women's track team headed by Edward Stanley Temple. Born in Harrisburg, Pennsylvania, September 20, 1927, Temple attended and graduated from TSU with a bachelor's and master's degrees in health and physical education. He took the women's program to national prominence within a few years after being appointed Head Coach at TSU, while at times using some personal funds.

His Tigerbelles, as they were known then and now, won 34 national titles, and his runners won 23 medals in international Olympic competition (13 gold, 6 silver, and 4 bronze).

Not only was Temple concerned with his team winning on the track, but he pushed them to devote themselves to their studies and earn their degrees. He noted that his greatest accomplishment was that of the 40 Tigerbelles he carried to the Olympics, 39 of them graduated—with 28 going on to earn their master's degrees and Ph.D.s. Included in this group of outstanding track stars are Mae Foggs, Barbara Jones, Wilmas Rudolph, Wyomia Tyus, Edith McGuire, Madeline Manning, Martha Hudson, Lucinda Williams, and Chandra Cheeseborough.

Temple was Head Coach for the 1960 and 1964 US Olympic Teams and was the Assistant Coach for the 1980 Pan American Games. He also served as Head Coach of the USA Junior Team in 1982 and 1986. For 44 years, 1950-1994, he coached the TSU women's track team and also served as an associate professor of sociology. He retired from full-time teaching and coaching at TSU in 1994.

He has been elected to the National Track and Field Hall of Fame, the Tennessee Sports Hall of Fame, TSU Hall of Fame, and the Ohio Valley Conference Hall of Fame. His autobiography *Only the Pure in Heart Survive* was published in 1980.

The Tigerbelles continued their upsurge by developing talented performers who participated with distinction on both the national and international scene. Over the years, the Tigerbelles have continued to perform and to win in some of the top track and field events, such as the Pan American Games and the Olympics.

Likewise, the basketball program continued to prosper. For eight seasons, the TSU Cagers played in all but two NCAA Division II South Regional tournaments. During those years of championship play, the team won the South Regional four times, finished second twice, third once, and fourth once. TSU also participated in NCAA championship play in 1963 and 1967. The TSU basketball team was UPI College Champion in 1961 and Associated Press Champion in 1972. A large number from both football and basketball players attained All-American status and a sizeable number of basketball and football players were drafted by the pros.

With all of these accomplishments, there was little surprise when TSU became one of the nation's leaders in football draftees by the professional teams. In 1971, the football team ranked third in the nation with a total of nine draftees. There was one season when the team had the distinction of having all five seniors on the squad drafted. During this same period of time, the TSU swimming, tennis and boxing teams were making outstanding accomplishments in their own fields.

As noteworthy as remembrances and well-deserved recognition of these championship teams are, it is very important not to forget the outstanding successes of those TSU athletic teams that preceded them. Many times when speakers are recounting and lauding the successes of previous teams, athletes, coaches and administrators, they often simply speak of the period of time between the 60s, 70s and later years. They frequently omit reaching back far enough (during the 40s and early 50s) in making reference as to when the athletic prowess really first started. Yes, without a doubt, the 60s and 70s brought excellent coaches, teams and individual performers onto the scene. However, it should never be forgotten when it really all began, nor should the individuals who engineered those early successful feats be forgotten.

As for my husband, he was one of those successful coaches during the early years as well as a successful Director of Athletics during the 60s and 70s. Of note is the fact that quite a significant letter was written to him by John Merritt, one of the exceptionally successful football coaches. In essence, Mr. Merritt stated in his letter that as his teams were propelled into championship play, their accomplishments would not have been possible if it were not for the Athletics Director's never ending support. This expression of support was with reference to attention given by my husband to such things as budget, scheduling, recruiting, facilities and the like. Over the years, this sentiment, I am sure, was shared by other coaches as they evaluated the reasons for their many successes.

National Associations (NCAA and NACDA)

Shortly after becoming TSU's Director of Athletics and in keeping with Dr. Davis' desire to propel the university into national and international prominence (even though this was not the most common thing being done in those days), my husband, for the next fifteen years, became a moving force in the affairs of the national associations.

He became a member of and served on key committees in the National Collegiate Athletic Association (NCAA) including the Special Committee on Infractions, the Administrative Committee for the National Youth Sports Program and the Committee on Reorganization. He also served on the College Division Basketball Committee for 8 years, and in 1975, he was named chairman of the NCAA Division II Basketball Tournament Committee. From 1971-1973, he served on the prestigious NCAA Council. In addition to his NCAA involvement, he was the second secretary for the National Association of Collegiate Directors of Athletics (NACDA) from 1970-1975. He also served on the Executive Committee of NACDA as third vice-president, and in 1977, he was inducted into the NACDA's Hall of Fame. Yes, Dr. Davis had tremendous vision. He knew that such involvement would bring prestige and honor to the university, and it did.

As my husband attended the various committee meetings, bowl games, and other events which were held in different states over the nation, I can remember having been fortunate enough to have traveled with him to a few of them. I can recall having been with Tubby in Shawnee on Delaware, in Pennsylvania; Excellcia Springs, Missouri; Fort Lauderdale, Florida; the University of Tennessee in Knoxville, Tennessee; Independence, Missouri; Evansville, Indiana; San Francisco, California; Gatlinburg, Tennessee; Hollywood, Florida; Las Vegas, Nevada; Miami Beach, Florida; Montreal, Quebec; Pasadena, California (Rose Bowl); San Diego, California; and Columbus, Ohio. After reviewing his NACDA secretarial notes, I recalled that he also traveled to Chicago, Minneapolis, Kansas City, Houston, Denver, New Orleans and Phoenix.

With the coaches under Gentry's administration and their teams winning such wide acclaim, they were called upon to participate in many bowl games and pre- and post-season events. These took place in different parts of the nation as well as outside of the United States. This resulted in additional travel and appearances for both the team members and the Athletics Director. Unfortunately, however, Tubby did not get the opportunity to travel out of the country with that exceptional track team to the Olympics and to other far away places where they competed and continued to excel.

His presence and the excellent performances of all wherever they were made a tremendous impact. The outstanding manner in which they presented themselves and the fact that they always made it known they were from Tennessee State University made them tremendous ambassadors for the university. Yes, the name of TSU became known all over the United States as well as internationally. This had been envisioned, and because it did happen, not only did its athletic accomplishments become widely-known but the school's academic programs were also enhanced and student enrollment was positively affected by such vast recognition.

Over the years my husband worked hard, giving 100 percent effort and time to his job. He enjoyed his work, and he accomplished a lot. But he had always looked forward to early retirement. He wanted to travel and see the United States, and he wanted to do it in a leisurely fashion. As he was in the process of deciding to really retire, I remember him saying:

> I always felt that when I gave up coaching that was the most difficult decision I ever made, but I have agonized over this decision even more.
>
> For me personally this school has provided a place where I was permitted to work, to grow professionally, and to share my talents. And above all, I shall be eternally grateful for having had the opportunity to work with my peers and with the fine men and women who were students attending Tennessee State University.

Even so, in keeping with his thoughts of early retirement, after having spent 27 years at Tennessee Sate University and after having served as an integral part of the athletic program, on May 17, 1976, my husband wrote a letter to the president of the university, Dr. Frederick S. Humphries, requesting that his retirement begin at the end of the annual leave period.

1961
Tennessee's New Athletics Director, Howard C. Gentry with his family, Howard, Jr., Carol and Mrs. Gentry.

1968
Ed Martin, (center), new coach of Tennessee A&I State University's basketball team, previews this year's schedule with Athletics Director Howard Gentry, left, and new assistant coach Don Corbett.

HOWARD C. GENTRY
*Director of Intercollegiate and Intramural
Athletics, Professor of Health, Physical
Education and Recreation*

EDWARD ALFRED MARTIN
*Head Basketball Coach
Associate Professor of Health, Physical
Education and Recreation*

A native of Columbus, Ohio, where he starred as a three-letter man in football, basketball, and track. Gentry played college football at Florida A&M under Big Bill Bell and the fabulous Jake Gaither. As a college player, he made All-SIAC and All-America as a tackle.

Following coaching stints at North Carolina A&T, and Central State University, he joined the Tennessee State coaching staff in 1949 as head line coach under the late Henry Arthur Kean.

In 1955, he succeeded Kean as head coach. During his brief coaching career, he amassed a total of 42 wins, 10 losses and 1 tie. He won a national championship in 1956 when he was named Coach of the Year. His teams won the Midwest Championship three times.

Mr. Gentry was elevated to the office of Director of Athletics in 1961 and immediately became active in the affairs of the NCAA. Currently, he is a member of the NCAA Council and is secretary to the National Association of Collegiate Directors of Athletics.

Born in Allentown two years before Charles A. Lindbergh flew solo across the Atlantic, Edward Alfred Martin, who starred in basketball and baseball at Allentown High School, was named head basketball coach at Tennessee State in 1968, following Harold Hunter. During prep school, Martin won varsity letters and a berth on Pennsylvania's All-State high school cage squad.

At North Carolina A&T College, where his baseball coach was the university's present Director of Intercollegiate and Intramural Athletics, Howard C. Gentry, Martin won four letters each in basketball and baseball. In his senior year, Martin was named All-Central Intercollegiate Athletic Association in basketball, was named his school's "All Around Athlete" and was selected to Who's Who Among Students in American Universities and Colleges.

NYSP helps youngsters

walk tall • talk tall • stand tall

MEMORANDUM

From the Desk of

JOHN A. MERRITT
Head Football Coach

Without your help, this would not have been possible.

Many thanks.

John A. Merritt

The TENNESSEAN
SPORTS
Page 17
SATURDAY
June 18, 1977

Who Has Best Record in Last 11 Years?
Surprise—It's TSU

Tennessee State Athletic Director Howard Gentry was presented with a plaque by Head Football Coach John Merritt during the TSU football banquet Friday night. The award was in recognition of Gentry's 25 years of service to the football program, as both coach and athletics director. In all, 10 awards were presented to TSU players and coaches during the gathering, which honored the 1974 Tigers, who had an 8-2 record this past fall.

Merritt praises Gentry

By DEBBIE GROOMS

"He took a lot of pride in his work. He was a person of very strong character and a man of great dignity and integrity."

These illustrious words of praise are dedicated to Howard Gentry Sr. from John Merritt, Head football coach here at TSU.

According to Coach Merritt, Howard Gentry had a great coaching career with the Tigers as an assistant coach and Head football coach and eventually want on to become Athletic Director.

Gentry is to be credited in engineering Tennessee State in to NCAA Membership and he has served on numerous NCAA committees.

Ed Temple (Tennessee A&I track coach), Howard Gentry (A&I athletic director), Ralph Boston (A&I track star) and Wayne Reeves (Director of Physical Plant) look over construction of the new rubberized track being installed at Tennessee A&I. The track will be ready in time for the Volunteer Games Friday and Saturday.

National Collegiate Division II Championship

Tournament Committee Has Tough Job of Selecting Teams for Annual Shootout

Committee sets tourney guidelines

HOWARD GENTRY
TENNESSEE STATE
(Chairman)

FLOYD WALKER
CENTRAL MISSOURI STATE

ANDREW LASKA
ASSUMPTION

THOMAS J. MARTIN
ROANOKE

News
BULLETIN

TENNESSEE A&I STATE UNIVERSITY
NASHVILLE, TENNESSEE
SEPTEMBER, 1967

CONSTRUCTION AND RENOVATION IN STADIUM

NYSP PARTICIPANTS 1962

National Youth Sports Program
An education from summer fun

A&I Athletes, Coach, and Awards Won

ATLANTA, Ga.—Tennessee State came in for a lion's share of the honors here Friday night at the annual awards banquet sponsored by the Atlanta Daily World and the 100 Per Cent Wrong club. With their awards are, left to right, Charles Walker, 1956 Tiger grid star, Head Football Coach Howard C. Gentry, Track Coach Edward S. Temple, Lucinda Williams, Mae Faggs, Isabelle Daniels, and Margaret Matthews

Tennessee State Athletes Bring Home Added Honors

ATLANTA, Ga. — Tennessee State added to its athletic honors here Friday night at the annual awards banquet sponsored by the Atlanta Daily World and the 100 Per Cent Wrong club.

Top honors went to Head Football Coach Howard C. Gentry, Track Coach Edward S. Temple, and Dr. W. S. Davis, Tennessee State President.

Gentry was named Coach of the Year in football and Temple was named Track Coach of the Year. Gentry's Tigers captured the Mid-Western football championship and several of Temple's girl track stars made last year's U. S. Olympic team. Dr. Davis was named Citizen of the Year.

The Tiger grid team also was honored as Negro national champions. Captain Leon Jamison and Charles Walker received the trophy denoting the honor. Tennessee State has twice been winner of the trophy and needs one more victory to retire it permanently.

Lucinda Williams, Mae Faggs, Isabelle Daniels, and Margaret Matthews of Tennessee State were honored for their selection to the U. S. Olympic team.

SYMBOLS OF CHAMPIONS

It takes superb leadership to build a tradition of success in competition.

Witness this impressive display of trophies won by Tennessee A & I State University—and the men who helped make it possible. Seated from left to right: John B. McClendon, Coordinator of Health and Athletics; Dr. Walter S. Davis, University President; Daniel G. Kean, Gulf Public Relations Representative; Howard C. Gentry, University Athletic Director.

Dan Kean's brother, the late Harry A. Kean, after whom Kean Hall is named, established one of the finest coaching records in collegiate athletics.

Gulf salutes the men of Tennessee State University for their proud tradition of victory.

GULF OIL CORPORATION

CHAPTER TWELVE
Retirement

"Your retirement represents the end of an era of tremendous contribution to excellence at this university. It will certainly be difficult to find a successor qualified to carry on the high caliber of professionalism you have brought to the athletic department of this university. You will be greatly missed by your many friends and colleagues." — *Dr. Humphries*

Having tremendous regard for my husband, Dr. Humphries met with him before granting the request. As I recall, they sat and discussed many of the happenings that had taken place during his tenure as the Athletics Director at TSU—most of which were very good, but some had been quite troubling. Nevertheless, they had dealt with them, and in most instances, they were adequately resolved.

Upon realizing that my husband was very serious about retiring, Dr. Humphries subsequently wrote a letter granting the request "with great regret." When the announcement of his retirement was made public, it was really, really a shock to the entire education and athletic communities. After all, he was only 55 years of age! And because of his good works and because of my husband's popularity, the press sought him out and numerous articles relative to his retirement came out in the newspapers. In one of the articles, he was asked to tell of some of the greatest highlights of his career at TSU. He told them that, of course, over the years it gave him a great sense of satisfaction to witness the successes of the athletic programs and the expansion of the athletic facilities. He further went on to say:

> I think perhaps the most individual exciting highlight of my career, however, was probably in 1956, my first year as Head Coach of football, when we went to Miami to play in the Orange Blossom Classic. Each year a game was played in that location between Florida A&M and the highest ranking team for the year among the black colleges and universities. Those games could have been compared to the Super Bowl games of today. My excitement centered around

the fact that my team was to play against my alma mater, and the Head Coach of that team was my old coach Alfonso Jake Gaither. After an exciting nip and tuck game, we defeated them 41-39. Our team was named the National Champions and I was named Coach of the Year! I shall always remember that game and the excitement which I felt while standing among the people in that crowded stadium. It was overwhelming.

However, while speaking of the satisfying and exciting highlights of his career while at TSU, my husband also told the press of a major disappointment which he experienced while serving as the Athletics Director. He told of his tremendous disappointment because of the failure of TSU to gain admittance into the Ohio Valley Conference. He lamented:

I recommended to the administration here that we try to gain admittance to the OVC on three different occasions, and we were never successful in being included. I had always felt that we should become affiliated in this way with schools in our geographical area and within our athletic caliber.

As I write this biography, I am happy to say that in 1986, even though it was a longtime coming, the university was finally admitted to the Ohio Valley Conference.

As the newspapers continued to report about the retirement of my husband, Dr. Humphries shared with them a statement which he had written in the letter to Gentry. It was this heart-warming, yet humbling statement that read:

Your retirement represents the end of an era of tremendous contribution to excellence at this university. It will certainly be difficult to find a successor qualified to carry on the high caliber of professionalism you have brought to the athletic department of this university. You will be greatly missed by your many friends and colleagues.

So, at the end of the summer session after attending and enjoying the departing activities that were given for him, my husband left Tennessee State University, his place of employment for 27 years. In that I had resigned, we almost immediately started preparation for the first of our long awaited leisure travel trips.

Travel

Tubby had done a lot of traveling, but as most of it was related to his work, there had been very little time for him to do otherwise. Upon occasion, he wished for more time to visit with family and friends, to visit points of interest along the way, to fish, and to generally just roam around and to relax. This he was now able to do as we traveled up through Kentucky and Ohio and up and down the east coast.

Upon returning to Nashville, it was well into the fall of the year and ex-coworkers, friends, and acquaintances were engaged in their various activities and job responsibilities. There were some times when I would observe my husband looking out of the window to the street where neighbors would be passing on their way to and from their jobs. At those times, it appeared that he was having mixed feelings about what he might really want to do with the rest of his life. However, as I recall, not much time passed before he became so engrossed in home, church, community, and civic activities that there was little time to think about anything else except planning for the next trip.

For many years he had spoken of wanting to purchase a motor home and to take vacations in it. But since all during his working years, he had rarely taken over a week or so from his various jobs for vacations. Consequently, most of the time, motor home vacations had not been practical. But now, at this time, he excitedly encouraged me to go with him shopping for a motor home. Truthfully, I was not too keen on the idea of vacationing in a motor home. But, he continued to encourage me that it would be a good enjoyable way to go. So, off I went with Tubby so we could shop for a motor home. It did not take long to look around and to settle on one—a mini-motor home—that seemed to be practical for us. Consequently, it was purchased one day and the next day we left Nashville! We took the southern route and headed for Los Angeles, California to visit our daughter Carol and her family. Needless to say, neither of us was at all motor home savvy. But with my husband's life having been one of possessing the courage to try new things (and having been successful in doing so), off we went—and there I sat beside him! Even though I may have had confidence in my husband and in his many skills and abilities, I relied also on my constant prayers that we would have a safe journey in this vehicle which was so new to him. Fortunately, we did have a wonderful, trouble-free trip, and it was the beginning of many other wonderful trips. I will always treasure the memories of them and of having had the opportunity to take them with my husband.

NYSP Evaluator

As in the past, wonderful opportunities continued to be offered to him. Before leaving Nashville to start the first motor home trip, the NCAA made contact with my husband, asking him to become one of the evaluators of the National Youth Sports Programs on a part-time basis. Remember, as before stated, this program had grown to be conducted on a very large number of campuses all over the United States. So, in reality, as the offer was accepted, it was like "icing on the cake." With the job requiring his presence on the various campuses, what better way would one have to "see the United States!" When it was possible for the schedule to be arranged for him to get from one site to the next by driving, he would happily pack us into the motor home and off we went!

In between the campus visits where he carried out his evaluating responsibilities, many times there were days when it was possible for us to travel to other cities and states. This gave us the opportunity to visit a large number of famous landmarks that we had only heard about and dreamed of seeing. So, yes, my husband did get the opportunity to do a lot of motor home traveling, and he did see a lot of the United States for he served as an evaluator of the NYSP for seven years. In addition to travel within the United States, we took other trips into parts of Canada as well as into and all across the northern tier of Mexico. It was upon returning from one of these trips that it was made known to me that a building on the campus of TSU was to be named in honor of my husband.

While participating in various activities at home and while continuing to travel, he was, many times, called upon to speak at functions in and out of the city. Recognizing his experience and expertise in the field of athletics, most times but not always, he was asked to speak on topics dealing specifically with athletics such as "What It Means to be an Athlete"; "The History of Sports at Tennessee State University"; "The Role of Sports in Improving Race Relations"; and "Blacks in Collegiate and Professional Sports—Opportunity or Exploitation." Some other such topics which he spoke on were the following: "The Importance of Black Colleges as a Valuable Resource"; "Today's Children, Our Next Generation"; "Opportunity for Leadership in the Next Generation"; and "Qualities of a Beautiful Woman." Because he could include so many examples of personal experiences in his speeches, the content as well as his sincere method of presenting it were received with genuine interest.

Interim Athletics Director

In 1986, after 10 years of retirement from Tennessee State University, my husband was asked to return to the university to serve as Interim Athletics Director. As he pondered the request, he said:

> It is with mixed emotions that I approach this assignment, for I have truly been enjoying my retirement. Nevertheless, I am honored that it is felt that I can be of further service to the university in general and the Department of Athletics in particular. So, I look forward to be again working with what I consider to be one of the most outstanding athletic programs in the country. Also, I look forward to working with its fine group of dedicated coaches.

Like years before, he delved into the work with great enthusiasm, and it was amazing the excitement that was generated by his return, even though just on a temporary basis. One of the newspaper headlines, in bold letters read, "Gentry's Back; TSU Applies to OVC." Dr. Peterson, the interim president, made the following statement:

> TSU is extremely fortunate that Mr. Gentry has agreed to accept this appointment. He is uniquely qualified, having successfully served as the TSU Athletics Director from 1961 until his retirement in 1976. Mr. Gentry is well respected throughout TSU, Nashville and national and international communities. We are confident he, again, will provide effective leadership to the TSU program as Acting Director.

Ohio Valley Conference (OVC)

When my husband arrived on the job, it was felt that he needed to do several important things. First, he had to prepare to receive the inspection teams from the Ohio Valley Conference as well as to communicate to segments of the students, faculty, staff, alumni, and community as to the values of such an affiliation.

This was not an easy task because there were people in the Department of Athletics as well as throughout the school and community who were skeptical as to the value of such an affiliation. Their skepticisms were primarily related to the fact that there would be disruption in the traditional scheduling of athletic teams from historically black colleges and universities. Also, with the disparities that had always existed between the OVC schools and TSU, it was felt that the OVC schools would have an unfair advantage over TSU in competitive events. I can remember Tubby spending long numbers of hours talking among his colleagues as well as among people in the community. This he did in an effort to encourage them to accept the possibility of OVC membership.

Second, he had to bring about improvements in the morale of the Department of Athletics, which had deteriorated in the past several years. Third, he needed to help complete an unsettled football schedule and to assist in attempting to make it a financial success. Finally, he had to orientate new staff members to their duties and responsibilities.

Even though the hours of work needed to get the job done were long, tiring, and sometimes frustrating, within the approximate eight months that he served as the Interim Director, each phase of the responsibilities was met with relative success. He especially welcomed his involvement regarding promotion of the value of membership in the Ohio Valley Conference, in that he had been active in supporting that effort as early as in the 1960s. He always felt that in time the advantages of being in the conference would outweigh the disadvantages. So to have again been active in that effort and for it to have come to pass, at that time, was another absolute joy for him!

Volunteerism

As I think back over those years and beyond, and as I now review the list of all the jobs and activities in which he was engaged, I am inclined to believe that Tubby was, indeed, one who lived a purpose driven life. He put forth 100 percent effort into carrying out the responsibilities of his different jobs. Likewise the same effort and enthusiasm was displayed as he proudly engaged in a vast number of volunteer activities. He was a member of many organizations and was an officer in most. For example, he was a trustee in his church and served as chairman of the Finance Committee. He was a member and served as president of the Optimist Club of Central Nashville. He was a life member of the NAACP. He was the Vice Chair of

the Board of Directors of First Baptist Church Capitol Hill Homes—a res-
idence that houses the elderly and the handicapped—and he was a member
of the Metropolitan School Attendance Review Board. He also served as
the chairman of the Nashville Auditorium Commission.

He served as secretary of the WDCN Telecommunications Advisory
Committee, and he was on the boards of the Northwest YMCA and of the
American Red Cross. Additionally, he served as the foreman of the
Davidson County Grand Jury. He was a member of the Urban League and
within it a member of the Elder Mentor Committee. He also was on the
Recreational and Cultural Committee of Model Cities and was a member
of the Civic Arena Study Committee. He was a member of the Nashville
Chapter of the National Coalition to Save Black Colleges.

My husband maintained strong ties with TSU. He served on the TSU
Hall of Fame Induction Committee and on the TSU Athletic Search
Committee. He was also chairman of a TSU athletic fund drive. Other clubs
and organizations in which he held membership were the Tiger Round Ball
Boosters, Ohio State Alumni Club, Tiger Pride Foundation, Big Blue Club,
the Sons of Africa, the Agora Assembly, a Couples' Club, and a Sportsman
Club, where he was president.

As can be assumed by the titles, each of the organizations had its particular area of interest, and my husband treated all with equal energy and
interest. However, those that had as a part of their mission to mentor and to
uplift the lives of deprived and needy youngsters were the ones that brought
the most absolute satisfaction and joy to my husband. As an example, he
was asked to go to a preschool to read to the youngsters and to serve as "a
Grandpa." Most of the children came from single-parent homes and had
experienced very little male presence. My husband just naturally made it a
point to show a great deal of love toward these children, and they, in turn,
would wrap their little arms around his legs and cling to him every chance
they got to do so. This delighted him as much as it did them. He was proud
to act as a loving Grandpa to them.

Illness

In order to bring the biography to an end, I am going to backtrack a bit.
In the midst of those years after retirement from TSU, in 1979, three years
after retirement, and upon having his yearly physical examinations, it was

discovered that Tubby had prostate cancer. That, of course, caused a great deal of concern among the few with whom he chose to share this situation. Being the caring person he was and not wanting to alarm a host of family members, friends and associates, he quietly went through the recommended periodic treatments, which initially covered about a month's period of time.

At times, there was discomfort caused by the treatments, but for the most part, he was able to continue to carry out previously accepted responsibilities without outwardly showing the pain. And, again, by the grace of God, there was remission of the cancer for 10 years. During those 10 years, however, in order to have constant knowledge of his condition, there had to be periodic visits to the doctor.

However, in 1989, my husband began to experience exceptional, terrific pain, different from arthritis pain which he had been bothered with over the years. As it turned out, upon having one of his usual periodic examinations, it was found that the cancer had returned. From that time, and for the next several years, he was treated with the very sophisticated procedures that were being recommended at that time.

Since it was necessary for him to remain in the hospital for longer periods of time than other times after treatment, a certain segment of the community became aware of his condition. You see, other times he would bounce back and continue with his usual activities, so it was not until the winter of 1994 when he finally was forced to become bedridden—that it became general knowledge that Howard Gentry, Sr. was seriously ill.

It was at this time that his doctor, privately, recommended to me that he should be placed on the Alive Hospice Program. Knowing that Tubby had, at all times, wanted to have complete knowledge of his condition, including its prognosis, I suggested to the doctor that his statement relative to the Alive Hospice should be made in the presence of my husband. This he did and after he left my husband's hospital room, I can remember that there passed some moments of somber silence among those of us present, which included our daughter Carol and our son Howard. I am sure that our thoughts were in concert, thinking about the fact that when one is on the Alive Hospice Program, it means that one's life is expected to end within a six month period of time. The first words that were spoken were those of my husband and his words led me to know that he, too, was thinking these same thoughts. His words were:

You know. I have previously said that I wanted the minister
who over the years has served as interim minister of our
church to preach my funeral, but I have changed my mind.
I want our present minister to preach my funeral because I
do not want to leave this world with the congregation feeling that I was promoting division among them.

Here, again, such a statement pinpoints the strong character of this man.
But to understand this statement, it has to be told that the present pastor had
been selected and had been serving for only a short period of time. And
within that period of time, differences had arisen between him and certain
persons within the various administrative bodies as well as within the general congregation of our church. My husband held respected positions
within the Trustee Board as well as other volunteer positions within the
church, and I am sure that in making the decision to have the present pastor of the church to preach his funeral, his thinking (even though he, too,
experienced differences) was geared toward the hope that in so doing, it
would help to bring the body of people closer together.

We Build People.

We're the YMCA.

Announcement Shocks Officials: No Successor Named

TSU's Gentry To Retire

By JEFF HANNA

Howard C. Gentry, director of athletics at Tennessee State University since 1961, announced yesterday he will retire from that position, effective July 1.

THE ANNOUNCE-MENT came without warning and shocked members of the athletic staff at Tennessee State where Gentry began as an assistant football coach in 1947.

"I always felt that when I gave up coaching that was the most difficult decision I ever made," said Gentry, 55. "But I have agonized over this decision even more.

"What prompted me to go in this direction at this time was a change in the retirement laws which makes it possible for me to retire," he added. "When a man works as hard as I have tried to work, you always look forward to that chance to retire. Now that I have that chance, I want to take it."

NO SUCCESSOR has been named. Dr. George Pruitt, said a committee has been appointed with Dr. George Cox, faculty chairman of athletics, as chairman.

"We hope to move with all due speed, but I have also coaxed Howard to remain with us until we have named someone," said Pruitt. "We are not far enough along to say whether there are any guidelines of any sort."

Pruitt did not indicate whether the selection committee would look at its present athletic staff for candidates, but there are indications that head football coach John Merritt looms as the likeliest candidate.

GENTRY IS a native of Columbus, Ohio, and a graduate of Florida A & M where he was an All-American offensive tackle under the legendary Jake Gaither.

He became assistant football coach at Tennessee State under the late

Howard Gentry
Surprise Announcement

Henry Arthur Kean in 1949 after serving on the staffs at North Carolina A & T and Central State.

In 1955, Gentry succeeded Kean as head football coach at State where his teams compiled a record of 42-10-1. He was elevated to director of athletics in 1961 and, in that position; has been extremely active in the NCAA, serving on the prestigious NCAA Council at one time.

UNDER GENTRY'S reign, State's athletic programs prospered with national champions in both football and basketball as well as unparalleled international successes in women's track and field.

"I think, perhaps, the highlight of my career was probably in 1956, my first year as head coach, when we went to the Orange Blossom Classic in Miami to play my alma mater, Florida A & M. and my old coach, Jake Gaither, and defeated them 41-39," said Gentry.

"Of course, I have also seen considerable progress over the years in our athletic programs and our facilities," said Gentry.

GENTRY SAID his
(Turn to Page 29)

(From First Sports Page)

major disappointment as athletic director as the failure of Tennessee State to gain admittance to the Ohio Valley Conference.

"I recommended to the administration here that we try to gain admittance to the OVC on three different occasions, and we were never successful," said Gentry. "I had always hoped that we would be able to become affiliated in this way with schools in our geographical area and within our athletic caliber.

"The consolation I have is the fact that our football schedule next fall includes Middle Tennessee, UT Martin and UT Chattanooga while the basketball team plays both Austin Peay and UT Martin," he added.

GENTRY SAID his decision to ask for the early

"The fact that the state has just apportioned $9 million for a new convocation center on our campus is one more instance of that growth."

retirement was based on something that Kean, the former head coach at State, told him.

"Back in 1952, Coach Kean talked me into this kind of thing," said Gentry. "One of the objectives as far as my lifetime has been was to be able to spend some time doing what I wanted to do."

Responding to his letter requesting the retirement, Tennessee State president Dr. Frederick S. Humphries wrote that Gentry's retirement "represents the end of an era of tremendous contribution to excellence at this university...It will certainly be difficult to find a successor qualified to carry on the high standards of professionalism you have brought to the Athletic Directorship of this University."

TSU's Howard Gentry, pictured here with his wife, is leaving the comfortable confines of retirement to aid the TSU fund raising effort.

Howard Gentry Named

TSU Launches $250,000 Fund

Ex-TSU Official Appointed To Auditorium Commission

Howard C. Gentr
nessee State Univer
rector, has been a
Metro Auditorium (

The appointment,
ard Fulton, must b
Metro Council.

FULTON SAID
"pleased Gentry ha
tribute his talent an
our community by
appointment to o
commission."

Gentry will fill a v
by the recent resigna
Johnson, who reques
be re-appointed to a

Gentry was affil:
TSU athletic depart
than 27 years. He ret
of athletics early in

He is now director
Youth Sports Progi
oversees youth spor
several cities, inclu
Birmingham, Cincin
ta.

Grand jury foreman appointed

KIRK LOGGINS
Staff Writer

Retired Tennessee State University
Athletic Director Howard Gentry will
serve as foreman of the September
term of the Davidson County grand
jury, whose members were selected
yesterday.

Criminal Court Judge Ann Lacy
Johns appointed Gentry as grand jury
foreman for a four-month term, but
picked the panel's members at ran-
dom from a pool of prospective
jurors.

Johns said she will explain the

Howard Gentry
Ex-TSU athletic director

GENTRY CITES SCHEDULING DIFFICULTY

House Committee Endorses OVC Membership for TSU

Tuesday/JUNE 3, 1986 • THE TENNESSEAN ● 3-C

SU awaits action on OVC entrance

The Board of Trustees
First Baptist Church Capitol Hill
(Howard Gentry, Chairman, Insert)

Dedication Committee planning for the dedication of Kelly Miller Smith Towers

Left to right: Ruth Warford, Howard Gentry, Clarence Worrell, J. Franklin Taylor, Chairman, Ruth Dennis, Kelly Miller Smith. Not pictured: Dr. S. O. Banks.

Brochure Committee
Left to right: Howard Gentry, Chairman, Augustus Bankhead, Cecille Crump, S. O. Banks, Clarence Worrell, L. Quincy Jackson, Mabel C. Boddie.

Helping preschoolers at Caldwell School

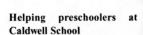

Grandpa Gentry

CHAPTER THIRTEEN
Final Days

"I'm fortunate to have had the support of my family—my wife, Carrie, and my children, Carol and Howie, my brothers and sisters, my church, and men like Bill Bell, Jake Gaither, Gaston (Country) Lewis and so many others who helped me along the way." — *Howard C. Gentry, Sr.*

Even though my husband's condition was as serious as it was, I knew that another preference of his was to be brought from the hospital to our home. That, too, was my desire. So, in consultation with his doctor and a head nurse with the Alive Hospice Organization, they decided it would be possible to have my husband brought to our home instead of having him being placed in a care center.

Along with the help of my husband's wonderfully devoted primary doctor, the exceptional group of people from the Alive Hospice Organization, the friends and people of the church and community as well as with our ever-present son and daughter, who over the years had experienced the love, devotion, and guidance of their father, we were able to care for my husband in our home. During the months that followed, of course, it was sad to see this 6'1", large-framed, previously active man unable to get out of bed without assistance. However, he never, even until the very last day, lost his ability to think or to converse. There were ministers and others who came by to visit with the thought in mind of comforting him. Some, however, said that upon occasion, there were times when it ended up with him ministering to them and comforting them. That was my husband!

The manner in which Tubby conducted his life indicated that throughout his adulthood he attempted to be guided by a spiritual belief. He was not in the habit of preaching on this subject. But frequently, a statement would be made by him, which would lead one to be aware of his belief. To exemplify this, I can recall a very simple but meaningful statement that he made while conversing with his minister who had come to visit with him on the last Christmas day that he was alive. We, the family, were seated around the dining table. It was customary for all to get together for a meal on Christmas Day, and my husband had been wheeled into the area and helped onto the couch. As he lay there conversing with the minister, I heard him say to the minister, "If He is ready for me to go, I'll go. But if He wants me to stay around a little longer, I'll stay." Obviously, as it turned out, God intended that he should remain around a bit longer for it was not until February 14, 1995, on Valentine's Day, that he died.

While he was bedridden, there were constant visitations by family and friends who made special trips from such far away places as California, Ohio, New York, Florida, Georgia, and Kentucky. He thoroughly enjoyed them all, but for his longtime friends and classmates, Hansel Tookes and Allen Killings, and for his friend from the army days, Jay Fiddler—for them to fly from Florida, Ohio, and New York, respectively, just for a few hours to visit with him, was very special. The love and respect that so many, from various walks of life, held for my husband was further shown by continuous visits from other longtime friends, former students, athletes, club and association members, church members, pastors, former co-workers, national organization members, and acquaintances in general.

Speaking of longtime friends and remembering some of the meaningful and caring things which they did still bring tears to my eyes. For example, with Valentine's Day approaching, one of those longtime friends, Jack Tarleton, came into the house with a Valentine's Day card, which had the heading "With Love to My Wife." He took it to Tubby, read its message for him, and then helped him to sign it. Jack knew without a doubt Tubby would have made the same choice of card with the same kind of loving message, and he wanted him to experience the joy of giving it.

A regular visitor was an old friend, Dr. Alvin Brown, a physical therapist who had recently relocated and made his home in Nashville. I mention him primarily because early on he was the person responsible for the proper examination and subsequent proper treatment being given—the results of which determined that my husband's pain was being caused by the cancer having returned and not from arthritis as was previously thought.

It so happened that Dr. Alvin "Boo" Brown was visiting one of the facilities where my husband was doing the recommended exercise that was thought to be the proper treatment to relieve the pain believed to be caused by the arthritis. However, as my husband told me, when Dr. Brown came into the room where he was and saw him experiencing such pain caused by the exercises, Dr. Brown said to the staff person, "What in the h— are you doing to that man?!"

Of course, the exercising was stopped, and then Dr. Brown came to the waiting area where I was seated and told me that I needed to have Tubby's doctor set up an appointment for him to have an MRI. This I did, and the results of the MRI showed that the old cancer had returned and metastasized. That knowledge, of course, changed the course of treatments which were given to my husband.

In between the treatments and for about four years, Tubby was able to go out to different activities and to visit with friends. Eventually, however, he became bedridden. It was during the time that my husband was bedridden that Dr. Brown would come and stay for long periods of time. He would browse through old albums and scrapbooks, and they would visit and catch up on the happenings that had taken place during the past years when they had been out of touch while living in different cities. Their reminiscing and his long visits were enjoyed and very much appreciated.

Another regular visitor, Reverend William Alexander, was a minister who pastored a church which was located just right over the hill from where we lived. He would visit our house and stand in my husband's room each day. He would not stay very long, and he would simply speak to my husband, give a few words of praise and leave. During the last few days of my husband's life, Reverend Alexander would just come in, touch him and then leave. Knowing that he would come around the same time each day, I would simply leave the door open so that he could just come on in.

The street on which our house was located formed a circle all around the hillside. From the first year that we moved into our newly-built home, we invited some of the residents who lived around the circle and several friends from other communities to come for a couple of hours for fellowship and a bowl of chili. This has taken place each Christmas Eve except for two. One was when our daughter's wedding reception was held there on December 23 and other activities connected with it spilled over into the next day. The other exception was 1994 when Tubby was bedridden. He really wanted us to go ahead with it, but Carol, Howie, and I decided not to do so.

But our wonderful neighbors did a most heartwarming thing. On that day, a group of them came into the house and brought with them a lovely decorated Christmas basket. In it was a card from each of those families.

Each had written words expressing their appreciation of Tubby's leadership to the community. They also specifically spoke of their appreciation of him bringing them together, face to face, to share the holiday spirit on Christmas Eve for more than three decades.

It may be of interest to tell of how the idea of the chili tradition first started. I can remember that it was a cold day on December 24, 1965. My husband made a big pot of chili, which he loved to do. On the evening of that day, Tubby and I were cozily sitting in front of a fire in our family-room. Out of the clear blue sky, he said, "Why don't we invite some of our friends over for a bowl of chili?" And we did! They gladly came, and we had a wonderful time. The next year, Tubby suggested that it would be great fellowship to invite all of the residents on the circle as well as the other friends from the community. And we did! He made a huge pot of chili. We invited them, they came, had a great time and this is how it started. Presently, my son and his family are continuing with the same Christmas Eve chili and fellowship activity which was started that cold winter evening 41 years ago.

During that last Christmas season of my husband's life, there continued to exist the loving attention and support of all. The support of individuals and groups was varied and extensive. The attention which they gave my husband was exceptional. I shall always remember them, and I will always be eternally grateful.

On the day of his death, Ed Martin, one of the men who my husband coached while on his first job at A&T College and who later became the Head Basketball Coach at TSU when my husband was the Athletics Director, came by for another visit. While there, communication existed between them, and in between, he fed my husband soup for his lunch. With such activity, one would never have guessed that later in the day he would take his last breath, but he did.

Subsequently, as preparation for my husband's funeral was underway, the support was outstanding. All of the things that customarily needed to be done preceding and during a funeral were simply done when those won-derful neighbors, members of the church, friends in the community and Tennessee State University stepped in and did them.

It was decided that a memorial service should be held in the Howard C. Gentry Center the day preceding the funeral. This was done and the serv-ice was absolutely beautiful and nostalgic, with most of the organizers and participants having been connected in some way with the university. They were from the administration, Academic Affairs, the Bureau of Public Relations, ROTC, the music department, as well as the former university minister, former coach/NCAA faculty representative, former basketball coach, and the captain of the 1956 National Championship TSU football team. In addition, there was the Associate Director for the NCAA, as well as a state Senator of the 19th District (a former student) and a state Representative of the 58th District (a former student). I feel that my husband was smiling from ear to ear for he loved them all.

On the next day for the funeral service, our church, First Baptist Capitol Hill, was packed and jammed—standing room only. I could not, at the time, determine who all of the people were, but later learned that there were people from all walks of life. They were people whose lives he had touched as well as people who had touched his life.

As expected, for the most part, the program participants were members of the church, including our son Howie. But, in addition to church members, a nephew whom we babysat who was now a minister practicing his profession in Pennsylvania also assisted with the service. And also on the program were a congressman, Bob Clement; a former coach, Ed Martin; and two presidents of Tennessee State University—Dr. Frederick Humphries and Dr. James Hefner.

After the burial at the National Cemetery in Madison, a suburb of Nashville, all gathered back at the church for visitation and a meal. Then it could be better seen who all had been in attendance. As I looked around, I could see that there was a large enough number of the Gentry family present for us to have had a family reunion like the one which had taken place yearly on the farm of Tubby's brother in Dublin, Ohio. Tubby and I had attended that reunion each year of our marriage. Likewise, there was an equally large number of relatives attending from my side of the family. Even though a sad circumstance had taken place, a feeling of joy crept into my spirit as I looked out among all of them. I thought about how, over the years, Tubby and I had happily embraced each other's families, as well as friends of our families. Many times we were called upon to open our doors to all—family, extended family, and friends—who might have been sent our way. As a matter of fact, our home was sometimes referred to as "The Gentry Hotel." It could always be seen that family and friend relationships meant a great deal to my husband and to me.

As I continued to look out over that gathering, it was overwhelming seeing so many from various and distant places. I especially want to mention one who came from Michigan—Mae Zimmerman. I learned that because of her job she could be away for only a very limited amount of time. But she said, "I was determined to be present at Mr. Gentry's funeral." She was a former TSU student who had lived with us and helped with our children, Carol and Howie. We, in turn, provided for her needs in order for her to be able to remain in school. She was like family for three years. She graduated, became a teacher and married, but she kept in touch and had never missed sending my husband a card on Father's Day.

While attending the memorial service, I noticed that several of the flowers spread over the casket had withered. So, later that afternoon, I called the undertaker and asked him if he would remove those which had withered and replace them with fresh red roses. I told him that it had been the practice of my husband to give me a dozen red roses on each of our wedding anniversaries. The next day when I entered the church for the funeral and looked at the closed casket, much to my surprise, the total spray of flowers on the casket was made up of beautiful live red roses!

A day or so later when I called the undertaker to say that I had only asked for several roses, but certainly intended to pay for all, I was told by him that he and his wife were giving the full spray of roses. He emphasized that they simply wanted to do that. Those wonderful friends were former students, Richard and Delorse Lewis.

I have mentioned some of the various persons, events, and occurrences because I want to re-emphasize the fact that my husband's past relationships with all people were of such that, even in sickness and in death, individuals were moved to act in positive, caring ways toward him. The many kind and caring acts that were bestowed upon my husband were absolutely humbling.

As I end my story of Howard C. Gentry, Sr.'s journey through life, I find myself wanting to spend more time reminiscing. The recollections and my writing about them have been such a pleasing thing to do—so much so that I just do not wish to stop! Nevertheless, I am forcing myself to end the writing. However, the memories are continuously running through my mind—memories about a life that Tubby shared with me for so many years. Thoughts about that life, which was of such an exceptional quality, I shall never wish to forget it. Memories about that life will always be treasured.

In the Introduction, I promised information to address the often asked question, "Why is that building named the Howard C. Gentry Complex?" I believe this book will benefit posterity and those who might have had the same question but did not ask. Most importantly though it is my hope that the information about my husband succinctly answers the question as to why a building on the campus of Tennessee State University has been named the Howard C. Gentry Health, Physical Education, Recreation and Convocation Complex.

I'd like to leave you with a quote from Tubby which I believe shows the spirit of humility that was always evident in him.

> I'm fortunate to have had the support of my family—my wife, Carrie, and my children, Carol and Howie, my brothers and sisters, my church, and men like Bill Bell, Jake Gaither, Gaston (Country) Lewis and so many others who helped me along the way.

These words, as well as other loveable characteristics which he possessed, will never leave my heart and I am sure will also remain in the memory of many others.

Tennessee State University says goodbye to a legend, Howard C. Gentry

Honoring a Tennessee State University legend

State Sen. Thelma Harper presents Carrie Gentry with a plaque honoring her husband, the late Howard Gentry. Watching the presentation, made in the Senate Chamber during Thursday's session, are Carol Gentry Johnson, Rep. Mary Pruitt and Howard Gentry Jr. The senior Gentry, a former football and athletic director at Tennessee State University, died last month.

Appendix A

O n the previous pages, the noteworthy qualities, characteristics and accomplishments of Tubby have been widely detailed. In addition, on the following pages, numerous memorial statements and copies of letters, as well as a listing of awards and recognitions that were provided by others, are presented. Without a doubt, these inclusions will likewise add to capturing the spirit of it all. Those who knew Tubby well have been unanimous in their praises of him.

The following statements were taken from daily newspapers, school newspapers and personal contacts.

Howard Gentry, Jr., son, TSU Athletics Director (1995)

He was a wonderful role model. By example, he basically taught me everything I know about athletics. He was a silent giant. He didn't boast a lot, but his actions were dominate. You could always go to the bank with anything he said or did. Relative to his legacy, I don't know if anyone will ever accomplish what he did. He told me that it was not an ivory tower position; it was a working job and the only way to succeed was to work and to do it in an honest and upstanding manner.

Carol Gentry Johnson, daughter

It has been said that it is better that something be caught rather than taught. When I think about my daddy, I recall it being said by many that he could be with princes or paupers, and he treated all the same. By his example, I caught on to the fact that everyone should be treated with dignity and respect regardless of their station in life. My daddy also taught me love for family which included extended family as well as dear friends. Most importantly, my daddy made it clear to my brother and me that he loved us dearly, but that his love for our mother surpassed even his love for us. What an example to emulate!

James Hefner, TSU President

The Tennessee State University family is saddened by the passing of Howard Gentry. He left an indelible mark at TSU. His contributions not only to the athletic success but also the overall excellence of the university will benefit countless future generations.

Dan Beebe, Ohio Valley Conference Commissioner

I wasn't here when he helped usher TSU into the OVC, but I understood the presence of the man and what he meant to TSU and to the NCAA in general. I can't think of anybody who demonstrated more class. He was the catalyst for Tennessee State moving to the OVC, and for that, we are all very grateful. Besides being an outstanding athletics administrator for a number of years, first and foremost, he was a great human being and a good friend of mine. He will be missed greatly.

Mrs. Ivanetta Davis, widow of the late Dr. Walter S. Davis, president of Tennessee A&I State College

Howard C. Gentry, Sr. was a handsome young football coach with a vibrant, beautiful wife when he joined the coaching staff at Tennessee A&I State College in 1949. My husband, the late Dr. Walter S. Davis, was the president of the college, and actively recruited and pursued Mr. Gentry because he had been genuinely impressed with the offensive line play of football teams coached by the young man. Mr. Gentry's abilities continued to impress my husband after he joined the coaching staff.

When it became necessary to select a new head football coach, after the era of Henry A. Kean, Coach Gentry was appointed to continue the winning tradition. Coach Gentry continued that tradition in grand style and produced a National Championship team that defeated a powerful Florida A&M team at the Orange Bowl in 1956. The game was played in Miami, Florida before a crowd of more than 45,000 spectators.

Coach Gentry was a great football coach, but my husband also recognized his vast potential to excel beyond the football field. He was selected by my husband to become the second Athletics Director at Tennessee State University. Coach Gentry's tenure as the Athletic Director was very successful and the athletic programs flourished. National championships were attained in basketball, football, swimming, and track. Coach Gentry's contributions to the university are legendary, and they are etched in the annals of TSU athletics.

Jim Delaney, Big Ten Commissioner

He had a great relationship within the state of Tennessee, both within the educational community and the athletic community. He was a good man who had great values. He always represented Tennessee State nationally on a high level. He was a true gentleman. He gave everyone a lot of respect, and he was treated with a great deal of respect.

Lendell Massengale, Tennessee A&T football team (1952-1956)

One of my coaches was Howard Gentry, Sr., whom I admired very much. I admired him both on and off the field. On the field he was a hard worker and he made you one, too, but he was fair and encouraging to his football players. While teaching us the skills, behavior and attitudes required to be winners on the field, he was also teaching us how to be winners in the field of life. He was a successful coach and led us to the National Championship in the 1956-57 season. Off the field he exemplified himself as a model one would want to emulate.

Ed Martin, TSU basketball coach

He was my coach, my teacher, but most of all, my friend. He was an inspiration to so many. He's been with me since I was 18 years old. Without him, I probably would not have gone to college. He recruited me to go to North Carolina A&T in 1948. He hired me to become TSU's basketball coach. He taught me so much about athletics and about life. He made a boy a man.

A lot of people did not realize what a great coach he was; they didn't realize what a great administrator he was. Gentry gave TSU so much credibility with the NCAA. He was so well respected with people in the NCAA. He was on the NCAA Committee at a time when not too many blacks were on those NCAA committees. He was the kind of guy who, when he stood up and spoke, everybody would listen to. The best way to describe him would be "Mr. Impact." When I was basketball coach and Ed Temple was track coach and John Merritt was football coach, we had some great years. He was a great Athletics Director for TSU. I've never seen a man who could work a budget like he could. When you needed money, somehow he could go to the cupboard and get it.

Tom Wood, sports writer for The Tennessean

The legacy of Howard C. Gentry, Sr., former football coach and Athletics Director, who died of prostate cancer Tuesday night at age 73, goes beyond a national black college championship and a namesake athletic complex. Mr. Gentry was also deeply committed to the student-athlete concept, was involved in community affairs, the NAACP, the NCAA and other collegiate committees. Besides serving on the prestigious NCAA Council, Mr. Gentry served as chairman of the NCAA Division II Basketball Tournament Committee and as secretary of the National Association of Collegiate Directors of Athletics. Mr. Gentry will always have a special place in the hearts of his former athletes and teammates.

Louis Spry, NCAA Associate Executive Director

Did anyone have anymore integrity than Howard Gentry? Once he determined the right course of action, he stood tall in the face of those who would try to dissuade him to take a different way. He was always one of the people that you respected, a man of high moral character and ethics. He always wanted to do the right thing.

Joe Gilliam Sr., TSU football coach

My knowledge of and association with Howard C. Gentry, Sr., whom I called Coach Gentry, covers a period of nearly fifty years. I first heard of Coach Gentry when he played football with one of my older brothers at Florida A&M University in Tallahassee, Florida. They both matriculated out of Ohio. Coach Gentry became an outstanding lineman at FAMU.

I followed Coach Gentry's coaching career through North Carolina A&I University where he worked with Coach Bill Bell, another FAMU great. Then on to Central State University in Wilberforce, Ohio where he worked for Coach "Country" Lewis. At these coaching stops, Coach Gentry developed the reputation of being one of the great line coach task masters at historically black colleges. This outstanding résumé garnered the attention of Coach Henry Arthur Kean at Tennessee A&I State College in Nashville, Tennessee and resulted in Coach Kean hiring Coach Gentry to handle the line at that college.

For the next three decades, Coach Gentry served as an extraordinarily successful head football coach and as an associate professor of physical education and as the Athletics Director at what is now called Tennessee

State University. During this era, Tennessee State University enjoyed unparalleled success in all sports, under the leadership of Howard C. Gentry in the capacity of the Athletics Director. There were successive national champions in basketball, football and swimming and national and Olympic champions in women's track under the tutelage of the legendary Ed Temple.

Coach Gentry's impact upon Tennessee State University was so overwhelming until the Educational Board of Regents of the State of Tennessee saw fit to name a huge structure on the campus in honor of Coach Gentry, named the Howard C. Gentry Complex. All of these significant honors were extremely apropos because we are talking of a man who walked with the giants of intercollegiate athletics in this country. Not only did he administer over this truly extraordinary athletic program at Tennessee State University, but he also served on the Executive Committee of the NCAA governing body. Howard C. Gentry, Sr., was always politically correct, administratively correct, culturally correct and socially correct. Howard C. Gentry, Sr., was an extraordinary human being.

Bernard Crowell, former coach and NCAA Faculty Representative

He was a molder of men and ideals. He made tireless efforts to keep the educational process and athletic achievements in the proper perspective. He did this with continuous efforts of dynamic leadership. He was a leader who knew the value of a quality education first and then winning attitudes and skills that led to national championships.

Eddie Robinson, Grambling State coach

Gentry was a great competitor. We had some fine games. He was such a fine guy, a fine coach, and a great person.

Dr. Hezekiah Foreman, TSU instructor for the physical education department and men's track coach

Gentry taught his players to take the high road through life. He influenced my life to have integrity and honesty. He was a hardworking and demanding coach, but a very nice gentleman. He always wanted us to do better, to never be satisfied. He stressed playing rough but clean. He was a great man.

Bill Davis, TSU football coach

It was a delight being in his presence. He epitomized what coaching is all about in terms of athletics, in terms of academics, in terms of being yourself. To talk to Mr. Gentry was just interesting.

Frankie Allen, TSU basketball coach

Mr. Gentry was one of the real fine people I met when I got here. Being relatively new to the campus, I recognized the impact he had on TSU which demonstrated his ability to be a man of vision. He was a guy who made you feel better about yourself.

Tom Normand, staff writer for the Nashville Banner

Mr. Howard C. Gentry, the retired Tennessee State University Athletics Director, was noted for leading the TSU football team to a 9-0 regular record and victory at the Orange Blossom Classic in 1956 in only his first year as Head Football Coach. In his six years at the helm of the Tigers, Mr. Gentry posted five winning seasons and one tying season for a career record of 42-10-1. Mr. Gentry's many accomplishments have been recognized but in 1980, TSU's new athletic complex was named the Howard C. Gentry Complex in his honor. In 1990, for his many contributions to the university, he received the Tiger Award sponsored by the *Nashville Banner*.

Joe Biddle, sports writer for The Tennessean

Tennessee State lost a giant this week when football coach and athletic director Howard Gentry, Sr. passed away after a long courageous battle against cancer. Gentry's finest moments may have come on the floor at the NCAA Convention where he excelled as an orator and voice of reason. He also stood firm when TSU joined the OVC Conference. There was a lot of opposition at the time against going into the league and giving up some traditional rivalries with predominately black institutions, but Gentry had the foresight to see the school's athletic programs, other than football, wouldn't survive if they were not associated with a conference. More importantly, Howard Gentry touched lives by his care, his warmth and his gentle touch.

Jerry Ingram, editor for TSU Meter

When Tennessee State University persuaded Howard C. Gentry, Sr. to come out of retirement to head the athletics program, they knew he would do an excellent job. The 65-year-old Gentry is always visible because he works hard. He came in most mornings around 8 a.m. to the building that is appropriately named the Howard C. Gentry Complex, and he doesn't depart until around 8 p.m. That's great dedication for a man who was supposed to be retired. Gentry still cares about the program he worked so hard to build. He is open and a very wise human being, who cares about the welfare of the athletes, coaches, the community and the student body at TSU.

Fred Russell, columnist for the Nashville Banner

Howard Gentry, long a stalwart figure in Tennessee State University athletics and prominent in NCAA affairs, is Nashville's inductee into the Tennessee State Hall of Fame. He's eminently worthy.

Joe Burris, sports writer for The Tennessean

Ohio Valley Conference Commissioner Jim Delaney has announced the conference has formed an administrative internship program named in honor of former TSU Athletics Director Howard Gentry. Delaney said the internship was named in honor of Gentry because of his numerous, lifelong contributions to intercollegiate athletics, to his coaching, and to his administrative work at TSU.

William G. Patton, Tennessee A&I University assistant coach

Coach Gentry said, "Don't just start something; learn to be a finisher."

Dr. Wilbur Suesberry, TSU football team co-captain

He was a wonderful man. As a coach, he was an exceptional individual, a tremendous leader who developed a lot of character in his players. He always stressed that football was part of what we were there for but that education was the most important thing. Coach Gentry has a lot of people he saw through the program, and I don't know anybody who would say anything derogatory about him. He was a tough taskmaster and wanted us to be very competitive. Some felt that he was a little hard on us, but I can honestly say that my life was enriched by a person who instructed me through those years and kept me on the straight and narrow. He understood my personality better than anyone else. He was like a father to me. The guys on the team used to tease me, saying I was his son.

Rev. Dewey Lamar Nichols

Back in the 1970s and 80s, Mr. Gentry established a recreation program for the congregation and retirees at First Baptist. Every Friday, he and Mrs. Gentry would have games in Sasser Hall. We'd look forward to Friday nights. We'd have checkers, dancing lead by Mrs. Gentry, ping pong, and bingo. Refreshments would be served afterward.

Hansel Tookes, longtime friend, FAMU's assistant football coach, FAMU Director of Athletics

Howard was a tremendous disciplinarian; he was dedicated to his job and had a burning desire to bring out the best in people. He was a man of character and a very dear friend. Howard was my best man in 1946. My wife passed, and when I remarried in 1990, he was my best man again."

Jack Tarleton, longtime friend

Howard "Tubby" Gentry, Sr., his family, my bride and I began our respective homes in Nashville, Tennessee in 1949.

Our having met that same year marked the beginning of a friendship between our families which deepened and blossomed over the years to the present. Tubby and I and our families shared our common experiences and family aspirations and learned from and strengthened each other in the process of achieving our respective objectives. We also enjoyed the pleasures of the social life we found in common. I personally admired Tubby's concept of the ideal family, his flawless integrity and honesty and his unstinting devotion to his professional and family duties. Most of all, perhaps, I observed his primary objective in his academic profession to build not only a great, successful athletic team as football coach at TSU but especially his determination to develop good character within each of his athletes and other students. I suspect that it was as much his success in this effort which accounted for the historic athletic successes of his teams as it was his superb athletic coaching skills.

These two attributes and achievements did not escape the notice of his athletic association, for Tubby was conscripted to become a rising member of its administration. His subsequent administrative and academic success became recognized not only at TSU but in the broader social, civic and church communities.

On a more personal note, Tubby and I enjoyed fishing together and traveling for same in his motor home. Our families also enjoyed visitations at his lakeside home and the occasions he took our family members water skiing. Our travels included Mexico and Hawaii. Finally, when his last illness was overtaking him, I remember that he was so disabled that I had to help him sign his name to the Valentine's card I had brought for him to give his loving wife Carrie on his last day, February 14th.

Ernie Minaya, longtime friend

In 1973, Tubby and I found that we shared mutual fondness for the outdoors. This was particularly true for fishing. It was on our second boat trip that I thought I knew him well enough to ask about his faith. Although, I am not a religious person and tend to be a bit cynical at times, it was my way of testing people regarding their sincerity.

He did not take my question lightly, and for a moment I was both his "pastor" and an old friend. Without hesitation he told me that God had been good to him. His life had started with nothing; yet today if you looked around you saw nothing but good things—a beautiful family, home, and respect in the community. He continued [by explaining that] without God none of this would have been possible.

I was taken by his sincerity and warmth. After all, this is not typical conversation for two men in the middle of the lake. It was the start of a great friendship.

James Buford, TSU football team captain (1956)

In those days, we did not call them role models, but he was one. He had the leadership qualities that you just gravitated to.

Samuel Abernathy, TSU associate professor

Mr. Howard Gentry was a phenomenal man who was a great supportive advocate. I was blessed to be a recipient of his philanthropy in several arenas, including football coach and Athletics Director at Tennessee State University as a mentor to the children at Caldwell Early Childhood Development Center where my daughter, Darlene, was a teacher, and as a member of the Optimist Club of Central Nashville, which he helped to organize in 1976 and served as the club's first president.

In all of these areas, Mr. Gentry exemplified the "fruits of the Spirit." His moral character and moral values were beyond reproach. He was always very professional, and yet he was kind, loving and patient. He had very high performance expectations for himself and for those with whom he worked.

Mr. Howard Gentry had a special gift for getting people to believe in themselves and to identify and bring out the best there was within them. He encouraged you to dream and to work hard to make your dreams a reality. One of my most memorable one-on-one experiences with him occurred one warm spring day when he stopped by my house while walking in the neighborhood. I was attempting to make a small repair at my house and was failing miserably, as usual. Mr. Gentry succeeded in convincing my disgusted wife that I was capable of performing the task; I simply didn't have the tools that I needed to do the job. He boosted my ego to the point that I went out and bought the tools that he told me to buy (and showed me how to use) and completed the job in a satisfactory manner. Even my wife was pleased; I was so very proud of myself, and my confidence in doing home repairs soared!

Life is better for so many people because of the positive seed that Mr. Howard Gentry planted in their lives. I thank God for this man of great faith; a teacher, advisor, encourager, role model and hero!

Dr. Keith Hagen, one of Gentry's physicians

In Robert Louis Stevenson's *Treasure Island*, he wrote, "We are all travelers in the wilderness of this world, and the best we can find in our travels is an honest friend." Wherever Howard Gentry traveled he carried this honesty. All who knew him understood this and because of this he earned the respect of all he encountered.

Warren C. Dance, TSU football team (1951-53)

Coach Gentry will not only be remembered by the games he won but also by the many lives he touched as a teacher, football coach and Athletics Director at TSU.

Joseph Simmons, TSU football team and student assistant

Coach Gentry and I came to TSU the same year, 1949. He was a hard and dedicated worker. Several players and I went to Coach Kean to see if we could talk him into getting rid of Coach Gentry because we felt that he was too rough and hard on us. Coach Kean listened to us. When we finished, Coach Kean said, "I wish I had two more like him." After my graduation in 1953, Coach Gentry started an intramural program, and I was his student assistant. This enabled me to get my master's degree in the summer of 1954. To show my respect for Coach Gentry, he was my first banquet speaker in Franklin, Tennessee. Coach Gentry was just what Dr. Davis said, "Always a class performance in deluxe style."

Stanley Gainer, TSU swim team

Coach Gentry was a serious-minded person who had a purpose in life and he was a team person. When necessary, he would help to transport the swimmers. Once when Coach Hughes, our swimming coach, had to be absent from a competition, Coach Gentry coached our team, and we won!

Paul Anderson, TSU football player (End, 1950; Tackle, 1951)

He was always a gentleman. He was respected for the manner in which he carried himself. We were not permitted to cuss. I always made sure that I did not stand next to him because when he called on one of us with which to demonstrate, he would knock you off your feet!

James "Biggie" Caldwell, TSU football team

Coach Howard Gentry, Sr. was like a daddy away from home to me. He was hard on me, but I found out that he loved me and respected me as an athlete. With his guidance, and his teaching me fundamentals of the game of football and life is the reason I received the honors of All-American, All-Midwestern, and the first lineman to be drafted by a professional football team (Chicago Bears, 1954). I just loved him and have nothing but the utmost respect for him as a man, a father, a coach, and above all, like my Daddy.

Fred Metcalf, TSU football team (1954 All-American Lineman)

Coach and Mrs. Gentry were like family to me. I was always proud to have Coach Gentry as my coach. He pushed us hard to be the best students and football players we could be. I have carried that determination throughout my life. I thank God that Coach Gentry touched my life as a young man.

Homer Wheaton, Associate Vice President for University Relations and Development

Howard C. Gentry, Sr. was a man with good character; he was loyal, had great vision, the ability to organize, develop programs, and lead a team toward desired goals. He was also an outstanding defensive and head football coach. However, in my opinion, Howard C. Gentry, Sr. should be first remembered for providing the leadership, as the Athletics Director, that made the athletics program at Tennessee State University one of the top programs in the nation in the college division. Tennessee State University should be extremely grateful to have had Howard C. Gentry, Sr. to lead its athletics program during a critical period in its development.

James Feathersone, Jr., TSU swim team

The endearing quality about Coach Gentry for me was the keen interest in my well-being and my academic performance. When I would see Coach Gentry on campus he would always ask, "Feather Merchant," (his nickname for me), "how are you doing? Are you keeping your grades up?" There are certain people in life who have a profound impact upon you. At Tennessee State, while meeting and learning from many fine individuals, Coach Gentry was one of them who had the most lasting impact.

Edward S. Temple, coach of the famous TSU Olympic Tigerbell track team

I have known Coach Gentry since 1949, the year that he came to TSU as the Head Football Line Coach under Henry Arthur Kean. I was a student at the time, but I graduated in 1950 and became coach of the women's track team. I was happy to bring him a topnotch football player by the name of Napoleon Holmes who excelled at TSU and played on Gentry's 1956 Championship team. Gentry became the Athletics Director in 1961 and served in that capacity until his retirement. Under his administration, the athletic teams continued to excel during those years.

Wayne W. Reeves, Director of Physical Plant Facilities

As Director of Physical Plant Facilities, I had the pleasure of working very closely with Howard Gentry, Sr. After he became Director of Athletics, I was always impressed with the strength of his character. His ideals and attitude were directed toward success. One of my most fulfilling and memorable design ventures was the Hale Stadium press box that was designed with Howard Gentry's assistance. He was a great guy!

No matter how taxing his day had been, Coach Gentry (as he was affectionately called) was always by my side as we made inspections of the athletic facilities prior to football and basketball games. He left the world better than he found it, and he will be remembered and missed on Tennessee State University's campus for a very long time.

John Bibb, sports editor at the Nashville Banner

Ever so often in this business, a sports writer happens to be in the right spot at the right time. You know, such as seeing Johnnie Wooden win his first of umpteen NCAA basketball championships, Bill Hagen limp up the hill at the 18th hole at August to win the Master's after his near fatal automobile accident, shivering on the sidewalk in South Bend watching a student pajama parade in the spitting snow on the eve of a Notre Dame football game, a Super Bowl kick-off, the final out of a World Series, teeing up for a round of golf on the Old Course at St. Andrews, cheering a glistening chestnut filly as she flashes home to win the Derby.

They are moments a guy never forgets.

The chills came again yesterday a few minutes after noon on the Tennessee State University campus. A stocky, bespectacled man stepped to the podium during a luncheon following the dedication of the new physical education and athletic building named in the honor of TSU's former Head Football Coach and Athletics Director, Howard C. Gentry.

The man's name is James Buford. He was captain of Gentry's 1956 TSU football team and now is Director of Human Services for the District of Columbia. What Buford had to say and the way he said it puts the tribute at the top of meaningful moments in the glorious world of sports.

James Buford, Captain of the 1956 championship football team and speaker at the dedication of the Howard C. Gentry Complex luncheon said:

> It is indeed a pleasure to have the opportunity to make a few remarks on the occasion of the dedication of the Howard C. Gentry complex. It is a pleasure not only because this complex memorializes the accomplishments of Howard Gentry but also because it affords the opportunity to convey to you some of the sentiments that I and many others share toward him.

> I met Howard Gentry in 1953—and for the past 27 years have known him as a student, an athlete, and as a very good friend. I did not want this opportunity to pass without paying all the tribute and offering all the respect and honor that I am capable of giving to Coach Gentry.

When I arrived on this campus in 1953, I was young, a little scared, determined to make good, and impressionable. The first person I really became attached to was Howard Gentry—I am not sure why because he was, in our opinion, a mean coach. Some of the guys called him crazy. But, I believe I must have spotted a weak spot and that attachment has lasted through the years.

In many ways, Howard Gentry was my role model—as a coach, as a true professional, as a family man and as a genuine human being. I have certain beliefs about the dimensions of the man that I would be proud to follow:

- He must be devoted to duty—he is of the people and toils on their behalf. There can be no soft spots in this demand, for a sense of duty is foremost and uncompromising.

- He must have courage—he must have enough steel in his spine so that the noisy dissent of the crowd doesn't sway him from what he truly believes to be the correct course to pursue.

- He must have a sense of fair play—he must at all times be insulated against arrogance, for the corrosion of power is both noticeable and noxious.

I share these personal thoughts with you because today we have come here to dedicate a monument to a man who has been a leader worthy of following—a man whose acceptance of duty, whose courage, whose appreciation for these virtues, however dimly reflected in others, have always been a natural part of him and his daily life. These are the qualities of heart and mind that I have, for almost thirty years, come to admire about Howard Gentry.

Howard Gentry has served this great institution with fidelity both to conscience and to pride—with ability and devotion.

As you well know, there are men and women who work each day to advance the progress of this institution. But in any institution, there are always a few who are doubters and who are faint-hearted. We know that doubters or the fearful cannot build institutions—it is always easy to declare why failure is certain and success is dim.

But what really lasts and endures and prospers is the work of the builder.

Wherever there is a collision with fate, when history stops for a moment of crisis, it is the doubter who runs from the test of courage, and it is the builder who is firm in the face of tremendous challenge.

And we, who know him, know that Howard Gentry has always been a builder of men and a builder of institutions.

I have never known Gentry to dwell on the minor imperfections that are always a part of human systems. He has always declared his faith in the hopes of this institution, and in the people who try to faithfully serve it.

We are here today to dedicate a monument to Howard Gentry. But, in a sense, we have arrived too late. Coach Gentry has built his own monument and built it long before the thought of the Gentry Complex rose in anyone's mind. His monument is the lives of those he coached, those he befriended and those he taught. That monument is already spread across the nation. Anything that we could build would be a lesser thing. We can only symbolize, in stone and glass and steel, what Coach Gentry has already built. But in doing so, we can proclaim our respect, our admiration and our pride in being numbered among his students, his colleagues and his friends.

Then, in a genuine sentimental moment, Buford presented Gentry with a prized memento of his coaching career. It was the game ball of that memorable 41-39 TSU victory over Florida A&M at the Orange Blossom Classic in Miami. As captain of the team, Buford had retained possession of the ball all these years.

By comparison, the long deflated football was a small gift delivered in the shadow of the magnificent $9 million structure that bears Gentry's name. But if anybody ever asks you how you get your name on the front of a building, tell him or her to call James Buford. Nobody ever said it better!

THE TOP AWARD Former Tennessee State athletic director Howard C. Gentry, Sr., left, receives the football from the 1956 TSU-Florida A&M game from James Buford, captain of the 1956 team that Gentry coached to the national black championship.

Editorial in The Meter

Howard Gentry, Sr., who led Tennessee State University to its most celebrated athletic moments, will be remembered as a builder—a builder of monuments through the lives of those he coached, taught and befriended across this nation. Coach Gentry was dedicated in his service to TSU and was very active in the community.

Appendix B

Honors and Recognitions

As can be seen by the following, many honors have been bestowed upon Howard C. Gentry, Sr.

1936	American Legion Varsity Appreciation Award
1937-38	All-City Tackle
1942	FAMU College Commission—Cadet officer
1943	All SIAC and All-American Team at FAMU
1956	Honorary Citizen of Empire of Texas
	Coach of the Year
1960	WVOL Citizen of the Day Citation
1966	TSU Student Council Proclamation
1967	Commendations from First Baptist Church—Capitol Hill for:
	Athletic coach-in-training, teaching of Negro youth on and off the field of play
	Inspiration and guidance which have contributed to human dignity among Negro athletes
	Christian image which leads athletes to Christ
1967	Scroll of Allegiance from Kappa Alpha Psi Fraternity for Dedicated Participation in Athletics
1972	Honorary Sergeant at Arms of the Tennessee House of Representatives

1973	NCAA Council
1976	Recognition Plaque from the TSU 1956 Championship Football Team
1977	NACDA Hall of Fame
	FAMU Sports Hall of Fame
	OVC Internships named in his honor
1979	TSU Homecoming Honoree
	TSU Outstanding Service Award
	Howard Gentry Day in Tennessee
1980	Howard C. Gentry Complex Dedication
	Midwest Official Association Award for Outstanding Service and Support
1981	TSU Big Blue Club Award for Outstanding Contributions to TSU Athletic Program and Nashville Community
1982	Black Expo Special Appreciation Award for Distinguished Community Service
1983	TSU Sports Hall of Fame
1984	Tiger Round Ball Booster Award
1984	Northwest YMCA Century Club Award
1986	TSU and Public Relations Honor for initiating NYSP on TSU Campus in 1969
	Mayor's Proclamation of Howard Gentry Day in Nashville
1987	Outstanding Graduate in Division of Health, Physical Education and Recreation at FAMU
1988	Ohio State university Alumni Club of Nashville Award for Outstanding Service to Education
	Optimist Club of Nashville Appreciation Award
	Honored by State of Tennessee House of Representatives
	Inducted into the Tennessee Sports Hall of Fame
	Inducted into the Tennessee General Assembly House Joint Resolution
1989	Mayor's Proclamation of Howard Gentry Day in Nashville
	State Senate Honorary Sergeant at Arms Certificate

1991	Kappa Alpha Psi Lifetime Achievement Award
	Honorary Chairperson of TSU Second Annual Alumni Scholarship Banquet
	Honorary Chairman, Torch Award Banquet
1992	Inauguration of Howard C. Gentry Athletic Endowed Scholarship Fund
	State of Tennessee House of Representative Honored 70th Birthday
1993	Most Admired Coach by Hubbard Alexander (TSU football player, 1956; professional coach, Dallas Cowboys)
	FAMU Graduate Recognition at 1993 Commencement
	Metropolitan Public Schools Good Friend Award for Volunteer Service during 92-93 school year
1995	Black Yellow Pages Remember—dedicated to Howard Gentry, Sr.
	Resolution Honoring Memory of Howard Gentry by the Senate of the State of Tennessee
1996	NCAA Memorial Resolution adopted at 90th Convention commemorating distinguished service
1997	Gen. Robert Neyland Award for Athletics Director (Posthumously)
	FAMU President Award (Posthumously)
	Forerunner Award (100 Black Men) (Posthumously)
1998	Induction into the West High School Alumni Association Hall of Fame (Posthumously)
2004	W. S. Davis Award
	Sportsman of the Week (*Banner Newspaper*)
	Columbus, Ohio Hilltop Community Recognition (Posthumously)

𝔉𝔞𝔶𝔢𝔱𝔱𝔢𝔳𝔦𝔩𝔩𝔢 𝔖𝔱𝔞𝔱𝔢 𝔘𝔫𝔦𝔳𝔢𝔯𝔰𝔦𝔱𝔶

FAYETTEVILLE, N. C.   28301

ESTABLISHED 1877

November 16, 1972

Mr. Howard C. Gentry
Director of Athletics
Tennessee State University
3500 Centennial Blvd.
Nashville, Tenn. 37203

Dear Tubby:

Thank you so very much for getting me the appointment as Chairman
of the NCAA Basketball Committee, South Atlantic area. I am
indeed happy and pleased to receive this and **grateful** to you for
it.

Please let me know the names of the people whom you have had in
the past, who were helpful members of that advisory committee.
I would like for them to work with me this year on your recom-
mendation.

Thank you again and I shall look forward to seeing you in Chicago
at the convention.

Sincerely yours,

William M. Bell
Director of Athletics

WMB/jew

Tennessee State University

Nashville, Tennessee 37203

OFFICE OF THE PRESIDENT

May 19, 1976

Mr. Howard C. Gentry
3502 Geneva Circle
Nashville, Tennessee 37209

Dear Howard:

    I have read your letter requesting that you be permitted to
retire from service to the University. With great regret your
request is granted. I had the opportunity to discuss your letter
and your retirement with Dr. Pruitt this morning. We both shared
the sentiment that your retirement represents the end of an era
in your tremendous contribution to excellence at this University.
You will be greatly missed by your many friends and colleagues.
It will certainly be difficult to find a successor qualified to
carry on the high standards of professionalism you have brought
to the Athletic Directorship of this University.

    I know the decision to leave an institution that has been
an integral part of your life for so many years was a difficult
one. Dr. Pruitt informs me that you have agreed to continue in
your present post until your successor has been named. Though I
know you have been looking forward to this moment for some time,
I am delighted that you consented to stay with us a little longer
so that the transition in leadership can be smooth and serve the
best interest of the University and the programs you have worked
so hard to develop. Be assured that you will always be a respected
member of the University Family and we look forward to enjoying
the benefits of your counsel in the years ahead.

    Take care and I wish you well.

Sincerely,

Frederick S. Humphries
President

FSH:ff

cc: Dr. G. A. Pruitt
    Dr. Bernard Crowell

TENNESSEE PUBLIC SERVICE COMMISSION
CORDELL HULL BUILDING
NASHVILLE, TENNESSEE 37219

OFFICE OF
BOB CLEMENT, COMMISSIONER
TELEPHONE 1 + 800-342-8359, EXT. 3668
AREA 615 741-3668 or 244-7381

June 1, 1976

KNOXVILLE OFFICE
AREA 615 522-7111

MEMPHIS OFFICE
AREA 901 534-6204

Mr. Howard C. Gentry
Athletic Director
Tennessee State University
Nashville, Tennessee 37200

Dear Mr. Gentry:

I would like to take this opportunity to wish you much happiness during your retirement. You have done an excellent job for Tennessee State University and the State of Tennessee.

If I can ever be of assistance to you, please feel free to contact me at any time.

Sincerely,

Robert N. Clement
Commissioner

RNC/d

You have much to be proud of —

June 14, 1976

Howard C. Gentry
Director of Athletics
TENNESSEE STATE UNIVERSITY
Nashville, Tennessee 37203

Dear Howard:

Just a quick note to acknowledge your recent letter.

Thank God I was sitting down when I read it or I
would have fallen over! Seriously, I would like
to offer my congratulations. Your early retirement
will be a severe blow to NACDA but I am sure best
for you and your family.

I'll look forward to talking to you about this in
Hollywood this weekend.

Kindest personal regards.

Sincerely,

Michael J. Cleary
Executive Director

MJC:cb

OLYMPIC YEAR · CANADA   1976   BICENTENNIAL YEAR · U.S.A.

11th
annual
convention
HOLLYWOOD, FLA. JUNE 21-23

RICHARD FULTON
MAYOR
METROPOLITAN COURTHOUSE
NASHVILLE. TENNESSEE 37201

July 29, 1976

Mr. Howard C. Gentry, Sr.
Director of Athletics
Tennessee State University
Nashville, Tennessee 37209

Dear Mr. Gentry:

        As you know, I was out of the city yesterday and was
unable to attend the banquet for this year's TSU National Youth
Sports Program. Joe Foster and Ann Chapman, from the office,
were able to attend on my behalf and both have told me how much
they enjoyed the luncheon.

        Joe, also, told me that you are now close to beginning
your retirement. I know this is something you have looked forward
to for months, and I hope that you and Mrs. Gentry will find the
great happiness each of you deserve in the years ahead. As I
have mentioned to you, however, our community cannot afford to
completely lose the services of your tremendous talents. In your
retirement years, I hope that Metropolitan Nashville will still
receive the benefits of these talents.

        With every good wish, I am

                        Sincerely,

                        RICHARD H. FULTON
                        Mayor

RHF:lw

TENNESSEE STATE UNIVERSITY
NASHVILLE, TENNESSEE 37203

Office of the Vice President
For Academic Affairs

May 24, 1976

Mr. Howard C. Gentry
Campus

Dear Mr. Gentry:

    I was genuinely sorry to hear of your retirement from Tennessee
State University as Athletic Director. My association with you over the
past years has been one of mutual concern for athletics and the students
whom we were charged with guiding, especially in the earlier years. You
will be sorely missed by faculty and staff here at TSU, and remembered
by the many young men whose lives you touched who were so much better
men because they had the privilege of your tutorage and guidance.

    Your consent to stay with us until a successor can be named and to
effect a smooth transition tells a lot about your character and concern for
the position even though you will be leaving. Fortunately for us you will
not be far away and we know that we can always depend on you for support.

    Again, Mr. Gentry, I am truly sorry to see you retire, and yet I
know how richly you deserve the privilege of making and keeping your own
schedule for a change, and enough time to do some of the things you have
wanted to do for pleasure for so long.

    With kindest personal regards, I am

                Cordially yours,

                Bernard G. Crowell
                Vice President for Academic Affairs

BGC:f

TENNESSEE STATE UNIVERSITY
NASHVILLE, TENNESSEE 37203

May 27, 1976

Radio Station WTSU
580 AM
Broadcasting on Campus

Mr. Howard C. Gentry
3502 Geneva Circle
Nashville, Tennessee   37209

Dear Howard:

When I received the news of your retirement my mind
immediately did a flashback through the years 1963 - 1976.

From 1963 - 1971 it was a real pleasure working with
you in the press box at the football games. There were
times when we had problems coordinating pre-game and half-
time activities, but I recall your quick action and diplomacy
in solving those problems. I told you then, and I'll say it
again, that the TSU press box was always the best organized
one in the entire circuit which I visited during my years
with the Aristocrat of Bands.

During the past four years, your cooperation and suggestions have been deeply appreciated in developing sports
programming at our campus radio station WTSU. The weekly
"Tiger Talks" is a successful program which gives a synopsis
of TSU athletic events and news. Most of the information for
these programs has come from your office.

The highlight of this year was the remote broadcasting
of the TSU basketball games from U-T Chattanooga and Kentucky-
Wesleyan in February. Through your meticulous planning we
were able to present our first two live remotes flawlessly.
When the radio station reaches its goal of becoming an FM
station and broadcasts into the city, we intend to broadcast
all TSU intercollegiate athletic events as you suggested in
many conversations with me.

It has been a privilege and a pleasure to have worked so
closely, and so rewardingly with you, with Mrs. Gentry (Band),
with Carol (Band), and with Howie (WTSU).

I wish you and your family the very best in the future.

In St. Paul's second epistle to Timothy, Chapter 4,
Verse 7, he wrote:

           "I have fought the good fight,
            I have finished the course,
            I have kept the faith."

Howard, so have you.

                              Sincerely,

                              Danny

                              Daniel E. Owens, Director
                              Radio Station WTSU

The National Collegiate Athletic Association

President	Executive Director	Secretary-Treasurer
J. NEILS THOMPSON	WALTER BYERS	EDGAR A. SHERMAN
University of Texas		Muskingum College
Austin, Texas 78712		New Concord, Ohio 43762

January 6, 1978

Mr. Howard C. Gentry
3502 Geneva Circle
Nashville
Tennessee 73209

Dear Howard:

The NCAA is most grateful for the contributions you and other
former members of the Council made to the development of this
Association.

The present Executive Committee has voted to present to you a
modest expression of their regard for the valuable services
you rendered to the NCAA and its Council during 1971-1973.

Recently, you should have received a plaque commemorating your
work with the Association. We did not anticipate the awards
company sending the plaque to your attention without providing
us with the opportunity to explain its intended purpose. Although this letter is after the fact, we hope it explains the
desire of the NCAA to express its thanks through the plaque for
your contributions and we hope it occupies a favored place in
your home or office.

Cordially yours,

Walter Byers

WB:dk

COMMITTEES:
APPROPRIATIONS
BUDGET
GOVERNMENTAL AFFAIRS

𝔘𝔫𝔦𝔱𝔢𝔡 𝔖𝔱𝔞𝔱𝔢𝔰 𝔖𝔢𝔫𝔞𝔱𝔢

WASHINGTON, D.C. 20510

October 19, 1979

Mr. Howard C. Gentry, Sr.
3502 Geneva Circle
Nashville, Tennessee   37203

Dear Coach Gentry:

It is certainly a pleasure for me to have
this opportunity of participating in these ceremonies
honoring you and your long and successful career as
Athletic Director and Coach at Tennessee State University.

Coach, you presided over a Golden Age of
athletics at Tennessee State University. The fame
and success of TSU continues, with its football players
starring on professional football teams throughout the
country. Tennessee State University under your leadership
has become known for its excellence in athletics as well
as in scholastics.

You are a star among stars, Coach, and I
certainly want to join your countless other friends
in commending and congratulating you on your fantastic
career and incredible record of success.

Sincerely,

Jim Sasser
United States Senator

BILL BONER
5TH DISTRICT
TENNESSEE

COMMITTEES:
PUBLIC WORKS AND
TRANSPORTATION
VETERANS' AFFAIRS

DISTRICT OFFICE:
552 U.S. COURTHOUSE
NASHVILLE, TENNESSEE 37203
615-251-5295

WASHINGTON OFFICE:
ROOM 118
CANNON HOUSE OFFICE BUILDING
202-225-4311

Congress of the United States
House of Representatives
Washington, D.C. 20515

October 22, 1979

Mr. and Mrs. Howard C. Gentry, Sr.
3502 Geneva Circle
Nashville, TN 37209

Dear Carrie and Coach Gentry:

This weekend was truly a great weekend. The weather could not
have been better, the parade was exciting, and the football game
was a climax to a successful weekend. However, the most important
of the weekend to me was the sharing in the program honoring
Howard C. Gentry, Sr. Participating in that service meant so much
to me. Not because I am the Congressman from the Fifth District,
but because the Gentrys have become such close personal friends of
mine.

A verse of scripture reads, "To him much is given of him will
much be required." Coach, you certainly have taken those abilities
that have been given to you and utilized them to their maximum.
I am convinced that no man can achieve the accomplishments in his
career and in his personal life and especially in his spiritual
life without the companionship of an outstanding woman.
While none of the plaques that were presented to you had the name
of Carrie Gentry engraved on them, knowing you like I do I am
certain that every one of those were accepted on behalf of both you.

I know that God will continue to bless both of you as you
look forward to many productive years in making a contribution to
our society.

Sincerely,

Bill Boner
Member of Congress

Office of the President
Tennessee State University
Nashville, TN 37203

October 14, 1980

Mr. Howard Gentry
3502 Geneva Circle
Nashville, Tennessee

Dear Mr. Gentry:

Congratulations on a well-deserved honor!

On September 26, 1980, the State Board of Regents acted upon a request from Tennessee State University which resulted in "Howard C. Gentry Health, Physical Education, Recreation, Athletic and Convocation Complex" as the name for our new multipurpose academic, convocation and sports facility.

The University is now making plans to dedicate the new facility. You can anticipate a letter from Mr. Sterlin Adams, Chairman of a University-wide committee I have appointed for the purpose of planning details of the dedication.

I look forward to seeing you in conjunction with this outstanding event.

Sincerely yours,

Frederick S. Humphries
President

FSH/w

ED MARTIN
HEAD BASKETBALL COACH

JOHNNY CAREY
ASST. BASKETBALL COACH

BASKETBALL   OFFICE

(615) 329-9500   Ext. 327

NASHVILLE, TENNESSEE 37203
October 3, 1980

Mr. Howard C. Gentry
3502 Geneva Circle
Nashville, TN

Dear Coach:

I tried to call you Saturday, but found out today that you are
out of town and won't return until Friday.

We were very elated with the new facility being named in your
honor. There is no doubt that you were very deserving. All one
has to do is check your track record.

We never gained national recognition until the administration
of Howard C. Gentry. When Howard C. Gentry spoke at the N.C.A.A.,
all listened. All this helped Tennessee State University. I only
hope my team can play up to the standards you always exemplified.

Congratulations!!

Yours truly,

Ed Martin
Head Basketball Coach

/p

JANE
ESKIND
CAMPAIGN
COMMITTEE,
Kent Harrell,
Treasurer

P.O. Box 1500,
Nashville, Tenn.
37202

Telephone:
615/320-1212

November 24, 1980

Mr. Howard C. Gentry
3502 Geneva Circle
Nashville, Tennessee 37209

Dear Howard:

Thanks so much for the invitation to join you, the TSU family, and your many friends at the dedication ceremony of the Gentry Complex, Tuesday, December 2nd. Nothing would give me greater pleasure than to be able to be there to help honor you as you have honored so many of us by your friendship and contributions to each of us for our community.

Nothing could keep me away except for the thousands of miles separating Nashville and Boston where I will be with Billy while he looks at colleges and they look at him (can you believe he is a senior already!).

Please take the will for the deed and know that I will be there in spirit.

My best to you, Carrie and the children.

Fondly,

Jane

JE:bsr

UNITED AMERICAN BANK
200 FOURTH AVENUE, NORTH
NASHVILLE, TENNESSEE 37219

November 25, 1980

Dr. Howard C. Gentry
3502 Geneva Circle
Nashville, Tennessee   37209

Dear Dr. Gentry,

To have a building named in your honor
is the reward for a life of service.
Please accept my heartfelt congratulations.

I will not be able to attend the dedication
ceremonies because I'll be out of town,
but hope to attend the Open House.

Again Congratulations.

Fondly,

JoAnn North

Mrs. William H. Andrews
2960 Ripley Road, Cleveland, Ohio 44120

Sunday
November 3, 1980

Dear Tubby,
    Just thrilled with the good
news. It pays to stick around
(smiles).
    So sorry we didn't hear
before yesterday. We probably
could have made it down
for the Dedication. Since its
just the two of us were always
off on 2 + three day junkies.
To tell Carrie I would have
been there to stick my chest
out with hers (smile)
    Come on up when you
can. Hello to all our mutual
friends
                    As Ever
                    Mildred + Billy

ARTHUR R. ASHE, JR.
369 LEXINGTON AVENUE
NEW YORK, NEW YORK 10017
(212) 687-1415

9 July 1984

Mr. & Mrs. Howard Gentry
3502 Geneva Circle
Nashville, Tennessee   37209

Dear Mr. Gentry:

What a sincere pleasure it was to have met and talked with you.
I still find myself amazed at the many accomplishments you have to your
credit, and I need not mention that much deserved building that sits in
your honor--it is overwhelming.

Also, thank you very much for allowing one of the better interviews
that I've done, and as soon as possible--probably in the next couple of
weeks--I will get a copy of it to you.

You have certainly aided in our project, and again thanks!

Sincerely,

Kip Branch

P.S.: I spoke with Zip Gayles

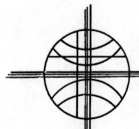

first baptist church, capitol hill

WALLACE CHARLES SMITH
PASTOR

615 - 255-8757

900 JAMES ROBERTSON PARKWAY
AT NELSON MERRY STREET
NASHVILLE, TENNESSEE 37203

May 7, 1986

Mr. Howard C. Gentry, Sr.
3502 Geneva Circle
Nashville, Tennessee 37209

Dear Mr. Gentry:

Just a note to congratulate you on your renewed responsibilities
as Tennessee State University Athletic Director.

With all that is going on at TSU top people are certainly needed
in key positions. I'm sure it was a difficult decision for you,
but I'm pleased that you accepted the challenge. All of us at
First Baptist will be praying for your continued success. If
I can personally do anything to help, let me know.

                              Sincerely yours,

                              Wallace Charles Smith
                              Pastor

WCS/jb

Department of Athletics
Tennessee State University
3500 John A. Merritt Blvd.
Nashville, TN 37209-1561

February 17, 1988

Mr. Howard C. Gentry, Sr.
3502 Geneva Cir.
Nashville, TN 37209

Dear Mr. Gentry:

     Congratulations on being inducted into the Tennessee Sports
Hall of Fame.

     Your success with the Tennessee State University Department of
Athletics and the National Collegiate Athletic Association have made
news across the country. I had the pleasure of working with you for
just a short time, but that timeframe was one of quality.

     Your induction into the Tennessee Sports Hall of Fame is quite
appropriate, and I am proud to have been associated with you.

     Again, congratulations and very best wishes.

                              Sincerely,

                              William Thomas
                              Athletic Director

/b

BILL BONER
STATE SENATE 18th DISTRICT

Mr. Howard Gentry, Sr.
3502 Geneva Circle
Nashville, TN. 37203

Dear Coach:

I recently learned that you were to be inducted into
the Hall of Fame at Florida A&M. I wanted to extend
my congratulations to you and let you know that I am
proud to say that I know such an outstanding person
such as yourself. I am enclosing an honorary Sergeant-
at-Arms certificate from the Tennessee State Senate
as my way of expressing my congratulations to you.

Sincerely,

Bill Boner
STATE SENATOR

BB/mp

*Congratulations
and Best Wishes*

Bobby Jones

Emma's Flowers and Gifts

BILL BONER
MAYOR
METROPOLITAN COURTHOUSE
NASHVILLE, TENNESSEE 37201

August 15, 1989

Mr. Howard Gentry
3502 Geneva Circle
Nashville, Tennessee   37209

Dear Howard,

I recently read that you have selected to serve as Foreman
of the September term of the Davidson County Grand Jury,
and I want to offer my personal congratulations for this
achievement.

The same determination and hard work that helped you win
this honor are qualities that make Nashville a great city.
I am personally proud of your success and wish you the very
best in your future endeavors.

Please feel free to call me or a member of my staff with
ideas or questions about how my office and all of Metro
Government can be of service to you.

Again, congratulations!

Sincerely,

Bill Boner
Mayor

⫷ Nashville Banner
1100 Broadway
Nashville, Tenn. 37203

Fred Russell
Vice President

PHONE: (615) 259-8219

Dec. 22, 1994

Dear Howard:

As I grow older (89) and
another Christmas approaches,
memories surge. When I think
of Januaries and the annual
NCAA covention, I remember my
good friend Howard Gentry as
one of the ablest, most respected
individuals in the history of
collegiate athletics.

Warm wishes,

Fred Russell

Appendix B   143

1OO BLACK MEN

April 24, 1997

Mrs. Carrie Gentry
3502 Geneva Circle
Nashville, Tennessee 37209

Dear Mrs. Gentry:

Each year the 100 Black Men of Middle Tennessee organization recognizes the contributions of distinguished individuals and organizations whose work has advanced the causes of our youth, particularly Black males.

These recognitions are made by presentation of awards at our Annual Dinner. Accordingly, I am pleased to inform you that your late husband, Howard C. Gentry has been named one of the recipients of our "Forerunner Award." **This award is given to individuals who were committed to the fulfillment of the mission of the 100 Black Men before the organization was founded.** Mr. Gentry's life work epitomized our mission of nurturing and enhancing the growth and development of young Black males.

The award will be presented at our Sixth Annual Dinner at Opryland Hotel on Saturday, May 17, 1997.

We would be pleased if you would be our special guest to receive this coveted award in honor of your late husband.

Please call me at 327-6774 or Quenton White at 292-9676, to confirm your acceptance of this award and for further details.

Sincerely,

Lloyd Elam
Chairman, Awards Committee

cc:
Samuel H. Howard
Quenton I. White

GENTRY FAMILY REUNION, DUBLIN, OHIO

HOWARD GENTRY FAMILY: Left to right: daughter, Carol; Howard, Sr.; Wife, Carrie; and son, Howard, Jr.

LaVergne, TN USA
14 October 2010

200705LV00003B/2/P